Spanish Verb Perfect

Fully Conjugated
Models For Every Type of
Spanish Verb
both regular and irregular

By: Peter Oakfield

Riverbridge Books

ISBN **978-1-9160398-0-3**

This edition published in the United Kingdom by
Riverbridge Books
192 Leckhampton Road, Cheltenham GL53 0AE   U.K.
Copyright © Peter Oakfield

About the author:
Peter Oakfield lives in the west of England and also writes about memory and topics related to the Spanish language. His other books include:

How to learn - Spanish - French - German - Arabic - any Foreign Language successfully.
 and
How To Transform Your Memory & Brain Power: Power-Learn, Memorize & Remember Anything.
and
How I Learned To Speak Spanish Fluently In Three Months: Discover How You Can Conquer Spanish Easily The Same Way.
and
Dual Language First Spanish Reader. Spanish-English Short Stories for Beginners
and
Dual Language Spanish Reader. Parallel Spanish-English Short Stories. Level Beginner to Intermediate
and
Spanish Verbs Genius: Everything you need to conquer Spanish Verbs and Speak Spanish correctly

comprar - buy
pagar -

tu
usted

Contents   Page No.
Introduction   4

Every Different Spanish Verb Type Fully   5
Conjugated

yo quiero estudiar
yo quiero escribir

ese that
esta this

{ Yo escribo.
{ necesito escribir en clase
{ yo estudio
{ necesito estudiar

Yo quiero leer

3

Introduction
Examples of Every Different Spanish Verb Type, both Regular and Irregular, Fully Conjugated

In this book you will find a fully conjugated example of every different type of Spanish verb, both regular and irregular. Study these fully conjugated verbs and you will find that you can conjugate every Spanish verb that you may ever, or can ever, encounter. With some of the verbs (e.g. stem changing verbs especially) 2 examples have been provided. In total there are 123 fully conjugated verbs.

With this book at your side you will have the perfect learning and reference aid to complete your command to the Spanish verb.

Accordingly this book is a companion volume to **Spanish Verbs Genius,** where you can learn about all the different Spanish verb types, their tenses and conjugations, and how to use them correctly. **Spanish Verbs Genius** also teaches you methods for mastering, memorising and recalling Spanish verbs and conjugations swiftly and efficiently.

Regular verb.

estudiar to study   son, Mi Perez

yo estudio
Tu estudias
Eu/Ella/Usted estudia   señor Perez

4

Every Different Type of Spanish Verb Fully Conjugated

All the model verbs you need to be able to conjugate any and every Spanish verb both regular and irregular.

Note: See also pages............ for additional comment regarding the Future, the Conditional and the Imperfect tenses.

Key to abbreviations:
R= Regular
O= Changes mostly Orthographic/Euphonic
S= Stem changes
RF= Reflexive
I= Irregular
M= Mixed changes/irregularities
Ú/Í= Stem U or stem I verb with stress changes
DC= Conjugation derived from some other verb
Past-P= Past-Participle
Pres P= Present-Participle
O/W = Otherwise
D= Defective, incomplete or impersonal verb. Only available in some conjugations.

List by category of verbs for which fully conjugated models are provided. (Alphabetical list below)

Models of fully conjugated Regular verbs

1-R-Hablar	2-R-Beber
3-R-Discutir	

Models of fully conjugated verbs with changes mostly Orthographic and/or Euphonic

4(a) & 4(b) -O-Bullir Empeller	5(a) & 5(b) -O-Bruñir & Tañer
6-O-Henchir	7-O-Rezar
8-O-Creer	9-O-Tocar

10-O-Pagar	11-O-Averiguar
12-O-Escoger	13-O-Dirigir
14-O-Distinguir	15-O-Delinquir
16-O-Vencer	17-O-Esparcir
18-O-Conocer	19-O-Lucir
20-M-Producir	21-O-Instruir
22-O-Argüir	23-O-Caer

Models of fully conjugated examples verbs with Stem changes

24(a) & 24(b) -S-Alentar & Acertar	25(a) & 25(b) -S-Perder & Entender
26(a) 26(a) -S-Aprobar & Acortar	27(a) & 27(b) -S-Morder & Remover
28-S-Oler	29(a) & 29(b)-S-Discernir & Cernir
30(a) & 30(b) -S-Sentir & Advertir	31(a) & 31(b) -S-Servir & Competir
32(a) & 32(b) -S-Adquirir & Inquirir	33(a) & 33(b) -S-Dormir & Morir
34-S-Jugar	35(a) & 35(b) -S-Reir & Freir
36(a) & (b)-S-Colegir & Elegir	

Models of fully conjugated Reflexive Verbs

37-R-RF-Abrirse	38-R-RF-Alejarse
39-I-RF-Caerse	40-S-RF-Convertirse
41-S-RF-Defenderse	42-S-RF-Despedirse
43-S-RF-Desvestirse	44-I-RF-Detenerse
45-O-RF-Dirigirse	46-S-RF-Divertirse
47-R-RF-Inscribirse	48-I-RF-Irse
49-R-RF-Levantarse	50-S-RF-Morderse
51-I-RF-Ponerse	52-S-RF-Reírse

53-S-RF-Sentarse	54-S-RF-Sentirse

Models of fully conjugated completely Irregular Verbs

55-I-Andar	56-I-Asir
57-I-Caber	58-I-Cocer
59-I-Dar	60-I-Decir
61-I-Errar	62-I-Estar
63(a)-I-Haber_& 63(b)-I-RF-Haber	64-I-Hacer
65-I-Ir	66-I-Oir
67-I-Poder	68-I-Poner
69-I-Querer	70-I-Roer
71-I-Saber	72-I-Salir
73-I-Satisfacer	74-I-Ser
75-I-Tener	76-I-Traer
77-I-Valer	78-I-Venir
79-I-Ver	

Models of fully conjugated verbs with mixed irregularities

80-M-Agorar	81-M-Almorzar
82-M-Avergonzar	83-M-Ceñir
84-M-Colgar	85-M-Comenzar
86-M-Empezar	87-M-Forzar
88-M-Regar	89-M-Seguir
90-M-Trocar	

Models of fully conjugated Uar, Iar, and stem U and stem I verbs with stress changes

91-Ú/Í-Evaluar	92-Ú/Í-Ampliar

93-Ú/Í-Aullar	94-Ú/Í-Airar
95-Ú/Í-Rehusar	96-Ú/Í-Prohibir
97-Ú/Í-Reunir	98-Ú/Í-Atraillar

Models of fully conjugated verbs with conjugation derived from some other irregular verb

99-DC-Deshacer	(same as Hacer) shown fully conjugated below
100-DC-Componer	(same as Poner) shown fully conjugated below
101-DC-Sobresalir	(same as Salir) shown fully conjugated below
102-DC-Equivaler	(same as Valer) shown fully conjugated below
103-DC-Retraer	(same as Traer) shown fully conjugated below
104-DC-Convenir	(same as Venir) shown fully conjugated below
105-DC-Prever	(same as Ver) shown fully conjugated below

Some Defective impersonal or limited Verbs:

106- D-R-S-Costar
107 D-R-Encantar
108-D-R-Gustar
109-D-S-Llover

Alphabetical list of verbs for which fully conjugated models are provided

Verb	No.		Verb	No.		Verb	No.
Abrirse	37		Deshacer	99		Oir	66
Acertar	24(b)		Despedirse	42		Oler	28
Acortar	26(b)		Desvestirse	43		Pagar	10
Adquirir	32(a)		Detenerse	44		Perder	25(a)
Advertir	30(b)		Dirigir	13		Poder	67
Agorar	80		Dirigirse	45		Poner	68
Airar	94		Discernir	29(a)		Ponerse	51
Alejarse	38		Discutir	3		Prever	105
Alentar	24(a)		Distinguir	14		Producir	20
Almorzar	81		Divertirse	46		Prohibir	96
Ampliar	92		Dormir	33(a)		Querer	69
Andar	55		Elegir	36(b)		Regar	88
Aprobar	26(a)		Empeller	4 (b)		Rehusar	95
Argüir	22		Empezar	86		Reir	35(a)
Asir	56		Encantar	107		Reírse	52
Atraillar	98		Entender	25(b)		Remover	27(b)
Aullar	93		Equivaler	102		Retraer	103
Avergonzar	82		Errar	61		Reunir	97
Averiguar	11		Escoger	12		Rezar	7
Beber	2		Esparcir	17		Roer	70
Bruñir	5 (a)		Estar	62		Saber	71
Bullir	4 (a)		Evaluar	91		Salir	72
Caber	57		Forzar	87		Satisfacer	73
Caer	23		Freir	35(b)		Seguir	89
Caerse	39		Gustar	108		Sentarse	53
Ceñir	83		Haber	63(a)		Sentir	30(a)
Cernir	29(b)		Haber RF	63(b)		Sentirse	54
Cocer	58		Hablar	1		Ser	74
Colegir	36(a)		Hacer	64		Servir	31(a)
Colgar	84		Henchir	6		Sobresalir	101
Comenzar	85		Inquirir	32(b)		Tañer	5 (b)
Competir	31(b)		Inscribirse	47		Tener	75
Componer	100		Instruir	21		Tocar	9
Conocer	18		Ir	65		Traer	76
Convenir	104		Irse	48		Trocar	90
Convertirse	40		Jugar	34		Valer	77
Costar	106		Levantarse	49		Vencer	16
Creer	8		Llover	109		Venir	78
Dar	59		Lucir	19		Ver	79
Decir	60		Morder	27(a)			
Defenderse	41		Morderse	50			
Delinquir	15		Morir	33(b)			

The Fully Conjugated Verbs

Regular AR verbs
1-R-Hablar

Verb infinitive	Participles	Imperfect-subjunctive 1
Hablar, to talk	hablado: hablando	yo hablara
		tú hablaras
Present	**Future**	él hablara
yo hablo	yo hablaré	nos'os habláramos
tú hablas	tú hablarás	vos'os hablarais
él habla	él hablará	ellos hablaran
nos'os hablamos	nos'os hablaremos	
vos'os habláis	vos'os hablaréis	**Imp'fect-sub've 2**
ellos hablan	ellos hablarán	yo hablase
		tú hablases
Imperfect	**Conditional**	él hablase
yo hablaba	yo hablaría	nos'os hablásemos
tú hablabas	tú hablarías	vos'os hablaseis
él hablaba	él hablaría	ellos hablasen
nos'os hablábamos	nos'os hablaríamos	
vos'os hablabais	vos'os hablaríais	**Imperative -Do**
ellos hablaban	ellos hablarían	(tú) habla
		(él) hable
Preterite	**Present subj've**	(nos'os) hablemos
yo hablé	yo hable	(vos'os) hablad
tú hablaste	tú hables	(ellos) hablen
él habló	él hable	
nos'os hablamos	nos'os hablemos	**Imperative-Don't**
vos'os hablasteis	vos'os habléis	no hables
ellos hablaron	ellos hablen	no hable
		no hablemos
Comp'nd tenses- 63-I-Haber +Past-P		no habléis
		no hablen

Regular ER verbs
2-R-Beber

Verb infinitive	Participles	Imperfect-subjunctive 1
Beber, to drink	bebido: bebiendo	yo bebiera
		tú bebieras
Present	**Future**	él bebiera
yo bebo	yo beberé	nos'os bebiéramos
tú bebes	tú beberás	vos'os bebierais
él bebe	él beberá	ellos bebieran
nos'os bebemos	nos'os beberemos	
vos'os bebéis	vos'os beberéis	**Imp'fect-sub've 2**
ellos beben	ellos beberán	yo bebiese
		tú bebieses
Imperfect	**Conditional**	él bebiese
yo bebía	yo bebería	nos'os bebiésemos
tú bebías	tú beberías	vos'os bebieseis
él bebía	él bebería	ellos bebiesen
nos'os bebíamos	nos'os beberíamos	
vos'os bebíais	vos'os beberíais	**Imperative-Do**
ellos bebían	ellos beberían	(tú) bebe
		(él) beba
Preterite	**Present subj've**	(nos'os) bebamos
yo bebí	yo beba	(vos'os) bebed
tú bebiste	tú bebas	(ellos) beban
él bebió	él beba	
nos'os bebimos	nos'os bebamos	**Imperative-Don't**
vos'os bebisteis	vos'os bebáis	no bebas
ellos bebieron	ellos beban	no beba
		no bebamos
Comp'nd tenses- 63-I-Haber +Past-P		no bebáis
		no beban

Regular IR verbs
3-R-Discutir

Verb infinitive	Participles	Imperfect-subjunctive 1
Discutir, to discuss, to argue	discutido: discutiendo	yo discutiera
		tú discutieras
Present	**Future**	él discutiera
yo discuto	yo discutiré	nos'os discutiéramos
tú discutes	tú discutirás	vos'os discutierais
él discute	él discutirá	ellos discutieran
nos'os discutimos	nos'os discutiremos	
vos'os discutís	vos'os discutiréis	**Imp'fect-sub've 2**
ellos discuten	ellos discutirán	yo discutiese
		tú discutieses
Imperfect	**Conditional**	él discutiese
yo discutía	yo discutiría	nos'os discutiésemos
tú discutías	tú discutirías	vos'os discutieseis
él discutía	él discutiría	ellos discutiesen
nos'os discutíamos	nos'os discutiríamos	
vos'os discutíais	vos'os discutiríais	**Imperative-Do**
ellos discutían	ellos discutirían	(tú) discute
		(él) discuta
Preterite	**Present subj've**	(nos'os) discutamos
yo discutí	yo discuta	(vos'os) discutid
tú discutiste	tú discutas	(ellos) discutan
él discutió	él discuta	
nos'os discutimos	nos'os discutamos	**Imperative-Don't**
vos'os discutisteis	vos'os discutáis	no discutas
ellos discutieron	ellos discutan	no discuta
		no discutamos
Comp'nd tenses-63-I-Haber +Past-P		no discutáis
		no discutan

4(a)-O-Bullir

Verb infinitive	Participles	Imperfect-subjunctive 1
Bullir: to boil, to stir	bullido: bullendo	yo bullera
		tú bulleras
Present	**Future**	él bullera
yo bullo	yo bulliré	nos'os bulléramos
tú bulles	tú bullirás	vos'os bullerais
él bulle	él bullirá	ellos bulleran
nos'os bullimos	nos'os bulliremos	
vos'os bullís	vos'os bulliréis	**Imp'fect-sub've 2**
ellos bullen	ellos bullirán	yo bullese
		tú bulleses
Imperfect	**Conditional**	él bullese
yo bullía	yo bulliría	nos'os bullésemos
tú bullías	tú bullirías	vos'os bulleseis
él bullía	él bulliría	ellos bullesen
nos'os bullíamos	nos'os bulliríamos	
vos'os bullíais	vos'os bulliríais	**Imperative-Do**
ellos bullían	ellos bullirían	(tú) bulle
		(él) bulla
Preterite	**Present subj've**	(nos'os) bullamos
yo bullí	yo bulla	(vos'os) bullid
tú bulliste	tú bullas	(ellos) bullan
él bulló	él bulla	
nos'os bullimos	nos'os bullamos	**Imperative-Don't**
vos'os bullisteis	vos'os bulláis	no bullas
ellos bulleron	ellos bullan	no bulla
		no bullamos
Comp'nd tenses-63-I-Haber +Past-P		no bulláis
		no bullan

4(b)-O-Empeller

Verb infinitive	Participles	Imperfect-subjunctive 1
Empeller, (o/w empellar) to push, to shove	empellido: empellendo	yo empellera
		tú empelleras
Present	**Future**	él empellera
yo empello	yo empelleré	nos'os empelléramos
tú empelles	tú empellerás	vos'os empellerais
él empelle	él empellerá	ellos empelleran
nos'os empellemos	nos'os empelleremos	
vos'os empelléis	vos'os empelleréis	**Imp'fect-sub've 2**
ellos empellen	ellos empellerán	yo empellese
		tú empelleses
Imperfect	**Conditional**	él empellese
yo empellía	yo empellería	nos'os empellésemos
tú empellías	tú empellerías	vos'os empelleseis
él empellía	él empellería	ellos empellesen
nos'os empelliamos	nos'os empelleríamos	
vos'os empellíais	vos'os empelleríais	**Imperative-Do**
ellos empellían	ellos empellerían	(tú) empelle
		(él) empella
Preterite	**Present subj've**	(nos'os) empellamos
yo empellí	yo empella	(vos'os) empelled
tú empellíste	tú empellas	(ellos) empellan
él empelló	él empella	
nos'os empellimos	nos'os empellamos	**Imperative-Don't**
vos'os empellísteis	vos'os empelláis	no empellas
ellos empelleron	ellos empellan	no empella
		no empellamos
Comp'nd tenses-63-I-Haber +Past-P		no empelláis
		no empellan

14

5(a)-O-Bruñir

Verb infinitive	Participles	Imperfect-subjunctive 1
Bruñir: to burnish	bruñido, bruñendo	yo bruñera
		tú bruñeras
Present	**Future**	él bruñera
yo bruño	yo bruñiré	nos'os bruñéramos
tú bruñes	tú bruñirás	vos'os bruñerais
él bruñe	él bruñirá	ellos bruñeran
nos'os bruñimos	nos'os bruñiremos	
vos'os bruñís	vos'os bruñiréis	**Imp'fect-sub've 2**
ellos bruñen	ellos bruñirán	yo bruñese
		tú bruñeses
Imperfect	**Conditional**	él bruñese
yo bruñía	yo bruñiría	nos'os bruñésemos
tú bruñías	tú bruñirías	vos'os bruñeseis
él bruñía	él bruñiría	ellos bruñesen
nos'os bruñíamos	nos'os bruñiríamos	
vos'os bruñíais	vos'os bruñiríais	**Imperative-Do**
ellos bruñían	ellos bruñirían	(tú) bruñe
		(él) bruña
Preterite	**Present subj've**	(nos'os)bruñamos
yo bruñí	yo bruña	(vos'os) bruñid
tú bruñiste	tú bruñas	(ellos) bruñan
él bruñó	él bruña	
nos'os bruñimos	nos'os bruñamos	**Imperative-Don't**
vos'os bruñisteis	vos'os bruñáis	no bruñas
ellos bruñeron	ellos bruñan	no bruña
		no bruñamos
Comp'nd tenses-63-I-Haber +Past-P		no bruñáis
		no bruñan

5(b)-O-Tañer

Verb infinitive	Participles	Imperfect-subjunctive 1
Tañer, to play (ie music/sound)	tañido: tañendo	yo tañera
		tú tañeras
Present	**Future**	él tañera
yo taño	yo tañeré	nos'os tañéramos
tú tañes	tú tañerás	vos'os tañerais
él tañe	él tañerá	ellos tañeran
nos'os tañemos	nos'os tañeremos	
vos'os tañéis	vos'os tañeréis	**Imp'fect-sub've 2**
ellos tañen	ellos tañerán	yo tañese
		tú tañeses
Imperfect	**Conditional**	él tañese
yo tañía	yo tañería	nos'os tañésemos
tú tañías	tú tañerías	vos'os tañeseis
él tañía	él tañería	ellos tañesen
nos'os tañíamos	nos'os tañeríamos	
vos'os tañíais	vos'os tañeríais	**Imperative-Do**
ellos tañían	ellos tañerían	(tú) tañe
		(él) taña
Preterite	**Present subj've**	(nos'os) tañamos
yo tañí	yo taña	(vos'os) tañed
tú tañiste	tú tañas	(ellos) tañan
él tañó	él taña	
nos'os tañimos	nos'os tañamos	**Imperative-Don't**
vos'os tañisteis	vos'os tañáis	no tañas
ellos tañeron	ellos tañan	no taña
		no tañamos
Comp'nd tenses- 63-I-Haber +Past-P		no tañáis
		no tañan

6-O-Henchir

Verb infinitive	Participles	Imperfect-subjunctive 1
Henchir: to fill	henchido: hinchendo	yo hinchera
		tú hincheras
Present	**Future**	él hinchera
yo hincho	yo henchiré	nos'os hinchéramos
tú hinches	tú henchirás	vos'os hincherais
él hinche	él henchirá	ellos hincheran
nos'os henchimos	nos'os henchiremos	
vos'os henchís	vos'os henchiréis	**Imp'fect-sub've 2**
ellos hinchen	ellos henchirán	yo hinchese
		tú hincheses
Imperfect	**Conditional**	él hinchese
yo henchía	yo henchiría	nos'os hinchésemos
tú henchías	tú henchirías	vos'os hincheseis
él henchía	él henchiría	ellos hinchesen
nos'os henchíamos	nos'os henchiríamos	
vos'os henchíais	vos'os henchiríais	**Imperative-Do**
ellos henchían	ellos henchirían	(tú) hinche
		(él) hincha
Preterite	**Present subj've**	(nos'os) hinchamos
yo henchí	yo hincha	(vos'os) henchid
tú henchiste	tú hinchas	(ellos) hinchan
él hinchó	él hincha	
nos'os henchimos	nos'os hinchamos	**Imperative-Don't**
vos'os henchisteis	vos'os hincháis	no hinchas
ellos hincheron	ellos hinchan	no hincha
		no hinchamos
Comp'nd tenses- 63-I-Haber +Past-P		no hincháis
		no hinchan

7-O-Rezar

Verb infinitive	Participles	Imperfect-subjunctive 1
Rezar: to pray	rezado: rezando	yo rezara
		tú rezaras
Present	**Future**	él rezara
yo rezo	yo rezaré	nos'os rezáramos
tú rezas	tú rezarás	vos'os rezarais
él reza	él rezará	ellos rezaran
nos'os rezamos	nos'os rezaremos	
vos'os rezáis	vos'os rezaréis	**Imp'fect-sub've 2**
ellos rezan	ellos rezarán	yo rezase
		tú rezases
Imperfect	**Conditional**	él rezase
yo rezaba	yo rezaría	nos'os rezásemos
tú rezabas	tú rezarías	vos'os rezaseis
él rezaba	él rezaría	ellos rezasen
nos'os rezábamos	nos'os rezaríamos	
vos'os rezabais	vos'os rezaríais	**Imperative-Do**
ellos rezaban	ellos rezarían	(tú) reza
		(él) rece
Preterite	**Present subj've**	(nos'os) recemos
yo recé	yo rece	(vos'os) rezad
tú rezaste	tú reces	(ellos) recen
él rezó	él rece	
nos'os rezamos	nos'os recemos	**Imperative-Don't**
vos'os rezasteis	vos'os recéis	no reces
ellos rezaron	ellos recen	no rece
		no recemos
Comp'nd tenses- 63-I-Haber +Past-P		no recéis
		no recen

8-O-Creer

Verb infinitive	Participles	Imperfect-subjunctive 1
Creer: to believe.	creído: creyendo	yo creyera
		tú creyeras
Present	**Future**	él creyera
yo creo	yo creeré	nos'os creyéramos
tú crees	tú creerás	vos'os creyerais
él cree	él creerá	ellos creyeran
nos'os creemos	nos'os creeremos	
vos'os creéis	vos'os creeréis	**Imp'fect-sub've 2**
ellos creen	ellos creerán	yo creyese
		tú creyeses
Imperfect	**Conditional**	él creyese
yo creía	yo creería	nos'os creyésemos
tú creías	tú creerías	vos'os creyeseis
él creía	él creería	ellos creyesen
nos'os creíamos	nos'os creeríamos	
vos'os creíais	vos'os creeríais	**Imperative-Do**
ellos creían	ellos creerían	(tú) cree
		(él) crea
Preterite	**Present subj've**	(nos'os) creamos
yo creí	yo crea	(vos'os) creed
tú creíste	tú creas	(ellos) crean
él creyó	él crea	
nos'os creímos	nos'os creamos	**Imperative-Don't**
vos'os creísteis	vos'os creáis	no creas
ellos creyeron	ellos crean	no crea
		no creamos
Comp'nd tenses- 63-I-Haber +Past-P		no creáis
		no crean

19

9-O-Tocar

Verb infinitive	Participles	Imperfect-subjunctive 1
Tocar: to touch, to play	tocado: tocando	yo tocara
		tú tocaras
Present	**Future**	él tocara
yo toco	yo tocaré	nos'os tocáramos
tú tocas	tú tocarás	vos'os tocarais
él toca	él tocará	ellos tocaran
nos'os tocamos	nos'os tocaremos	
vos'os tocáis	vos'os tocaréis	**Imp'fect-sub've 2**
ellos tocan	ellos tocarán	yo tocase
		tú tocases
Imperfect	**Conditional**	él tocase
yo tocaba	yo tocaría	nos'os tocásemos
tú tocabas	tú tocarías	vos'os tocaseis
él tocaba	él tocaría	ellos tocasen
nos'os tocábamos	nos'os tocaríamos	
vos'os tocabais	vos'os tocaríais	**Imperative-Do**
ellos tocaban	ellos tocarían	(tú) toca
		(él) toque
Preterite	**Present subj've**	(nos'os) toquemos
yo toqué	yo toque	(vos'os) tocad
tú tocaste	tú toques	(ellos) toquen
él tocó	él toque	
nos'os tocamos	nos'os toquemos	**Imperative-Don't**
vos'os tocasteis	vos'os toquéis	no toques
ellos tocaron	ellos toquen	no toque
		no toquemos
Comp'nd tenses-63-I-Haber +Past-P		no toquéis
		no toquen

10-O-Pagar

Verb infinitive	Participles	Imperfect-subjunctive 1
Pagar: to pay	pagado: pagando	yo pagara
		tú pagaras
Present	**Future**	él pagara
yo pago	yo pagaré	nos'os pagáramos
tú pagas	tú pagarás	vos'os pagarais
él paga	él pagará	ellos pagaran
nos'os pagamos	nos'os pagaremos	
vos'os pagáis	vos'os pagaréis	**Imp'fect-sub've 2**
ellos pagan	ellos pagarán	yo pagase
		tú pagases
Imperfect	**Conditional**	él pagase
yo pagaba	yo pagaría	nos'os pagásemos
tú pagabas	tú pagarías	vos'os pagaseis
él pagaba	él pagaría	ellos pagasen
nos'os pagábamos	nos'os pagaríamos	
vos'os pagabais	vos'os pagaríais	**Imperative-Do**
ellos pagaban	ellos pagarían	(tú) paga
		(él) pague
Preterite	**Present subj've**	(nos'os) paguemos
yo pagué	yo pague	(vos'os) pagad
tú pagaste	tú pagues	(ellos) paguen
él pagó	él pague	
nos'os pagamos	nos'os paguemos	**Imperative-Don't**
vos'os pagasteis	vos'os paguéis	no pagues
ellos pagaron	ellos paguen	no pague
		no paguemos
Comp'nd tenses- 63-I-Haber +Past-P		no paguéis
		no paguen

11-O-Averiguar

Verb infinitive	Participles	Imperfect-subjunctive 1
Averiguar: to ascertain	averiguado: averiguando	yo averiguara
		tú averiguaras
Present	**Future**	él averiguara
yo averiguo	yo averiguaré	nos'os averiguáramos
tú averiguas	tú averiguarás	vos'os averiguarais
él averigua	él averiguará	ellos averiguaran
nos'os averiguamos	nos'os averiguaremos	
vos'os averiguáis	vos'os averiguaréis	**Imp'fect-sub'ive2**
ellos averiguan	ellos averiguarán	yo averiguase
		tú averiguases
Imperfect	**Conditional**	él averiguase
yo averiguaba	yo averiguaría	nos'os averiguásemos
tú averiguabas	tú averiguarías	vos'os averiguaseis
él averiguaba	él averiguaría	ellos averiguasen
nos'os averiguábamos	nos'os averiguaríamos	
vos'os averiguabais	vos'os averiguaríais	**Imperative-Do**
ellos averiguaban	ellos averiguarían	(tú) averigua
		(él) averigüe
Preterite	**Present subj've**	(nos'os) averigüemos
yo averigüé	yo averigüe	(vos'os) averiguad
tú averiguaste	tú averigües	(ellos) averigüen
él averiguó	él averigüe	
nos'os averiguamos	nos'os averigüemos	**Imperative-Don't**
vos'os averiguasteis	vos'os averigüéis	no averigües
ellos averiguaron	ellos averigüen	no averigüe
		no averigüemos
Comp'nd tenses-63-I-Haber +Past-P		no averigüéis
		no averigüen

12-O-Escoger

Verb infinitive	Participles	Imperfect-subjunctive 1
Escoger: to choose	escogido: escogiendo	yo escogiera
		tú escogieras
Present	**Future**	él escogiera
yo escojo	yo escogeré	nos'os escogiéramos
tú escoges	tú escogerás	vos'os escogierais
él escoge	él escogerá	ellos escogieran
nos'os escogemos	nos'os escogeremos	
vos'os escogéis	vos'os escogeréis	**Imp'fect-sub've 2**
ellos escogen	ellos escogerán	yo escogiese
		tú escogieses
Imperfect	**Conditional**	él escogiese
yo escogía	yo escogería	nos'os escogiésemos
tú escogías	tú escogerías	vos'os escogieseis
él escogía	él escogería	ellos escogiesen
nos'os escogíamos	nos'os escogeríamos	
vos'os escogíais	vos'os escogeríais	**Imperative-Do**
ellos escogían	ellos escogerían	(tú) escoge
		(él) escoja
Preterite	**Present subj've**	(nos'os) escojamos
yo escogí	yo escoja	(vos'os) escoged
tú escogiste	tú escojas	(ellos) escojan
él escogió	él escoja	
nos'os escogimos	nos'os escojamos	**Imperative-Don't**
vos'os escogisteis	vos'os escojáis	no escojas
ellos escogieron	ellos escojan	no escoja
		no escojamos
Comp'nd tenses- 63-I-Haber +Past-P		no escojáis
		no escojan

23

13-O-Dirigir

Verb infinitive	Participles	Imperfect-subjunctive 1
Dirigir: to guide	dirigido: dirigiendo	yo dirigiera
		tú dirigieras
Present	**Future**	él dirigiera
yo dirijo	yo dirigiré	nos'os dirigiéramos
tú diriges	tú dirigirás	vos'os dirigierais
él dirige	él dirigirá	ellos dirigieran
nos'os dirigimos	nos'os dirigiremos	
vos'os dirigís	vos'os dirigiréis	**Imp'fect-sub've 2**
ellos dirigen	ellos dirigirán	yo dirigiese
		tú dirigieses
Imperfect	**Conditional**	él dirigiese
yo dirigía	yo dirigiría	nos'os dirigiésemos
tú dirigías	tú dirigirías	vos'os dirigieseis
él dirigía	él dirigiría	ellos dirigiesen
nos'os dirigíamos	nos'os dirigiríamos	
vos'os dirigíais	vos'os dirigiríais	**Imperative-Do**
ellos dirigían	ellos dirigirían	(tú) dirige
		(él) dirija
Preterite	**Present subj've**	(nos'os) dirijamos
yo dirigí	yo dirija	(vos'os) dirigid
tú dirigiste	tú dirijas	(ellos) dirijan
él dirigió	él dirija	
nos'os dirigimos	nos'os dirijamos	**Imperative-Don't**
vos'os dirigisteis	vos'os dirijáis	no dirijas
ellos dirigieron	ellos dirijan	no dirija
		no dirijamos
Comp'nd tenses- 63-I-Haber +Past-P		no dirijáis
		no dirijan

14-O-Distinguir

Verb infinitive	Participles	Imperfect-subjunctive 1
Distinguir:	distinguido, distinguiendo	yo distinguiera
		tú distinguieras
Present	**Future**	él distinguiera
yo distingo	yo distinguiré	nos'os distinguiéramos
tú distingues	tú distinguirás	vos'os distinguierais
él distingue	él distinguirá	ellos distinguieran
nos'os distinguimos	nos'os distinguiremos	
vos'os distinguís	vos'os distinguiréis	**Imp'fect-sub've 2**
ellos distinguen	ellos distinguirán	yo distinguiese
		tú distinguieses
Imperfect	**Conditional**	él distinguiese
yo distinguía	yo distinguiría	nos'os distinguiésemos
tú distinguías	tú distinguirías	vos'os distinguieseis
él distinguía	él distinguiría	ellos distinguiesen
nos'os distinguíamos	nos'os distinguiríamos	
vos'os distinguíais	vos'os distinguiríais	**Imperative-Do**
ellos distinguían	ellos distinguirían	(tú) distingue
		(él) distinga
Preterite	**Present subj've**	(nos'os) distingamos
yo distinguí	yo distinga	(vos'os) distinguid
tú distinguiste	tú distingas	(ellos) distingan
él distinguió	él distinga	
nos'os distinguimos	nos'os distingamos	**Imperative-Don't**
vos'os distinguisteis	vos'os distingáis	no distingas
ellos distinguieron	ellos distingan	no distinga
		no distingamos
Comp'nd tenses- 63-I-Haber +Past-P		no distingáis
		no distingan

25

15-O-Delinquir

Verb infinitive	Participles	Imperfect-subjunctive 1
delinquir to transgress, to sin	delinquido: delinquiendo	yo delinquiera
		tú delinquieras
Present	**Future**	él delinquiera
yo delinco	yo delinquiré	nos'os delinquiéramos
tú delinques	tú delinquirás	vos'os delinquierais
él delinque	él delinquirá	ellos delinquieran
nos'os delinquimos	nos'os delinquiremos	
vos'os delinquís	vos'os delinquiréis	**Imp'fect-sub've 2**
ellos delinquen	ellos delinquirán	yo delinquiese
		tú delinquieses
Imperfect	**Conditional**	él delinquiese
yo delinquía	yo delinquiría	nos'os delinquiésemos
tú delinquías	tú delinquirías	vos'os delinquieseis
él delinquía	él delinquiría	ellos delinquiesen
nos'os delinquíamos	nos'os delinquiríamos	
vos'os delinquíais	vos'os delinquiríais	**Imperative-Do**
ellos delinquían	ellos delinquirían	(tú) delinque
		(él) delinca
Preterite	**Present subj've**	(nos'os) delincamos
yo delinquí	yo delinca	(vos'os) delinquid
tú delinquiste	tú delincas	(ellos) delincan
él delinquió	él delinca	
nos'os delinquimos	nos'os delincamos	**Imperative-Don't**
vos'os delinquisteis	vos'os delincáis	no delincas
ellos delinquieron	ellos delincan	no delinca
		no delincamos
Comp'nd tenses- 63-I-Haber +Past-P		no delincáis
		no delincan

16-O-Vencer

Verb infinitive	Participles	Imperfect-subjunctive 1
Vencer, to conquer	vencido: venciendo	yo venciera
		tú vencieras
Present	**Future**	él venciera
yo venzo	yo venceré	nos'os venciéramos
tú vences	tú vencerás	vos'os vencierais
él vence	él vencerá	ellos vencieran
nos'os vencemos	nos'os venceremos	
vos'os vencéis	vos'os venceréis	**Imp'fect-sub've 2**
ellos vencen	ellos vencerán	yo venciese
		tú vencieses
Imperfect	**Conditional**	él venciese
yo vencía	yo vencería	nos'os venciésemos
tú vencías	tú vencerías	vos'os vencieseis
él vencía	él vencería	ellos venciesen
nos'os vencíamos	nos'os venceríamos	
vos'os vencíais	vos'os venceríais	**Imperative-Do**
ellos vencían	ellos vencerían	(tú) vence
		(él) venza
Preterite	**Present subj've**	(nos'os) venzamos
yo vencí	yo venza	(vos'os) venced
tú venciste	tú venzas	(ellos) venzan
él venció	él venza	
nos'os vencimos	nos'os venzamos	**Imperative-Don't**
vos'os vencisteis	vos'os venzáis	no venzas
ellos vencieron	ellos venzan	no venza
		no venzamos
Comp'nd tenses- 63-I-Haber +Past-P		no venzáis
		no venzan

17-O-Esparcir

Verb infinitive	Participles	Imperfect-subjunctive 1
Esparcir, to scatter	esparcido: esparciendo	yo esparciera
		tú esparcieras
Present	**Future**	él esparciera
yo esparzo	yo esparciré	nos'os esparciéramos
tú esparces	tú esparcirás	vos'os esparcierais
él esparce	él esparcirá	ellos esparcieran
nos'os esparcimos	nos'os esparciremos	
vos'os esparcís	vos'os esparciréis	**Imp'fect-sub've 2**
ellos esparzen	ellos esparcirán	yo esparciese
		tú esparcieses
Imperfect	**Conditional**	él esparciese
yo esparcía	yo esparciría	nos'os esparciésemos
tú esparcías	tú esparcirías	vos'os esparcieseis
él esparcía	él esparciría	ellos esparciesen
nos'os esparcíamos	nos'os esparciríamos	
vos'os esparcíais	vos'os esparciríais	**Imperative-Do**
ellos esparcían	ellos esparcirían	(tú) esparce
		(él) esparza
Preterite	**Present subj've**	(nos'os) esparzamos
yo esparcí	yo esparza	(vos'os) esparcid
tú esparciste	tú esparzas	(ellos) esparzan
él esparció	él esparza	
nos'os esparcimos	nos'os esparzamos	**Imperative-Don't**
vos'os esparcisteis	vos'os esparzáis	no esparzas
ellos esparcieron	ellos esparzan	no esparza
		no esparzamos
Comp'nd tenses-63-I-Haber +Past-P		no esparzáis
		no esparzan

28

18-O-Conocer

Verb infinitive	Participles	Imperfect-subjunctive 1
Conocer, to know	conocido: conociendo	yo conociera
		tú conocieras
Present	**Future**	él conociera
yo conozco	yo conoceré	nos'os conociéramos
tú conoces	tú conocerás	vos'os conocierais
él conoce	él conocerá	ellos conocieran
nos'os conocemos	nos'os conoceremos	
vos'os conocéis	vos'os conoceréis	**Imp'fect-sub've 2**
ellos conocen	ellos conocerán	yo conociese
		tú conocieses
Imperfect	**Conditional**	él conociese
yo conocía	yo conocería	nos'os conociésemos
tú conocías	tú conocerías	vos'os conocieseis
él conocía	él conocería	ellos conociesen
nos'os conocíamos	nos'os conoceríamos	
vos'os conocíais	vos'os conoceríais	**Imperative-Do**
ellos conocían	ellos conocerían	(tú) conoce
		(él) conozca
Preterite	**Present subj've**	(nos'os) conozcamos
yo conocí	yo conozca	(vos'os) conoced
tú conociste	tú conozcas	(ellos) conozcan
él conoció	él conozca	
nos'os conocimos	nos'os conozcamos	**Imperative-Don't**
vos'os conocisteis	vos'os conozcáis	no conozcas
ellos conocieron	ellos conozcan	no conozca
		no conozcamos
Comp'nd tenses-63-I-Haber +Past-P		no conozcáis
		no conozcan

19-O-Lucir

Verb infinitive	Participles	Imperfect-subjunctive 1
Lucir, to shine	lucido: luciendo	yo luciera
		tú lucieras
Present	**Future**	él luciera
yo luzco	yo luciré	nos'os luciéramos
tú luces	tú lucirás	vos'os lucierais
él luce	él lucirá	ellos lucieran
nos'os lucimos	nos'os luciremos	
vos'os lucís	vos'os luciréis	**Imp'fect-sub've 2**
ellos lucen	ellos lucirán	yo luciese
		tú lucieses
Imperfect	**Conditional**	él luciese
yo lucía	yo luciría	nos'os luciésemos
tú lucías	tú lucirías	vos'os lucieseis
él lucía	él luciría	ellos luciesen
nos'os lucíamos	nos'os luciríamos	
vos'os lucíais	vos'os luciríais	**Imperative-Do**
ellos lucían	ellos lucirían	**Imperative-Do**
		(tú) luce
Preterite	**Present subj've**	(él) luzca
yo lucí	yo luzca	(nos'os) luzcamos
tú luciste	tú luzcas	(vos'os) lucid
él lució	él luzca	(ellos) luzcan
nos'os lucimos	nos'os luzcamos	**Imperative-Don't**
vos'os lucisteis	vos'os luzcáis	no luzcas
ellos lucieron	ellos luzcan	no luzca
		no luzcamos
Comp'nd tenses-63-I-Haber +Past-P		no luzcáis
		no luzcan

20-M-Producir

Verb infinitive	Participles	Imperfect-subjunctive 1
Producir, to produce	producido: produciendo	yo produjera
		tú produjeras
Present	**Future**	él produjera
yo produzco	yo produciré	nos'os produjéramos
tú produces	tú producirás	vos'os produjerais
él produce	él producirá	ellos produjeran
nos'os producimos	nos'os produciremos	
vos'os producís	vos'os produciréis	**Imp'fect-sub've 2**
ellos producen	ellos producirán	yo produjese
		tú produjeses
Imperfect	**Conditional**	él produjese
yo producía	yo produciría	nos'os produjésemos
tú producías	tú producirías	vos'os produjeseis
él producía	él produciría	ellos produjesen
nos'os producíamos	nos'os produciríamos	
vos'os producíais	vos'os produciríais	**Imperative-Do**
ellos producían	ellos producirían	(tú) produce
		(él) produzca
Preterite	**Present subj've**	(nos'os) produzcamos
yo produje	yo produzca	(vos'os) producid
tú produjiste	tú produzcas	(ellos) produzcan
él produjo	él produzca	
nos'os produjimos	nos'os produzcamos	**Imperative-Don't**
vos'os produjisteis	vos'os produzcáis	no produzcas
ellos produjeron	ellos produzcan	no produzca
		no produzcamos
Comp'nd tenses- 63-I-Haber +Past-P		no produzcáis
		no produzcan

31

21-O-Instruir

Verb infinitive	Participles	Imperfect-subjunctive 1
Instruir, to instruct	instruido: instruyendo	yo instruyera
		tú instruyeras
Present	**Future**	él instruyera
yo instruyo	yo instruiré	nos'os instruyéramos
tú instruyes	tú instruirás	vos'os instruyerais
él instruye	él instruirá	ellos instruyeran
nos'os instruimos	nos'os instruiremos	
vos'os instruís	vos'os instruiréis	**Imp'fect-sub've 2**
ellos instruyen	ellos instruirán	yo instruyese
		tú instruyeses
Imperfect	**Conditional**	él instruyese
yo instruía	yo instruiría	nos'os instruyésemos
tú instruías	tú instruirías	vos'os instruyeseis
él instruía	él instruiría	ellos instruyesen
nos'os instruíamos	nos'os instruiríamos	
vos'os instruíais	vos'os instruiríais	**Imperative-Do**
ellos instruían	ellos instruirían	(tú) instruye
		(él) instruya
Preterite	**Present subj've**	(nos'os) instruyamos
yo instruí	yo instruya	(vos'os) instruid
tú instruiste	tú instruyas	(ellos) instruyan
él instruyó	él instruya	
nos'os instruimos	nos'os instruyamos	**Imperative-Don't**
vos'os instruisteis	vos'os instruyáis	no instruyas
ellos instruyeron	ellos instruyan	no instruya
		no instruyamos
Comp'nd tenses- 63-I-Haber +Past-P		no instruyáis
		no instruyan

22-O-Argüir

Verb infinitive	Participles	Imperfect-subjunctive 1
Argüir, to argue	argüido: arguyendo	yo arguyera
		tú arguyeras
Present	**Future**	él arguyera
yo arguyo	yo argüiré	nos'os arguyéramos
tú arguyes	tú argüirás	vos'os arguyerais
él arguye	él argüirá	ellos arguyeran
nos'os argüimos	nos'os argüiremos	
vos'os argüís	vos'os argüiréis	**Imp'fect-sub've 2**
ellos arguyen	ellos argüirán	yo arguyese
		tú arguyeses
Imperfect	**Conditional**	él arguyese
yo argüía	yo argüiría	nos'os arguyésemos
tú argüías	tú argüirías	vos'os arguyeseis
él argüía	él argüiría	ellos arguyesen
nos'os argüíamos	nos'os argüiríamos	
vos'os argüíais	vos'os argüiríais	**Imperative-Do**
ellos argüían	ellos argüirían	(tú) arguye
		(él) arguya
Preterite	**Present subj've**	(nos'os) arguyamos
yo argüí	yo arguya	(vos'os) argüid
tú argüiste	tú arguyas	(ellos) arguyan
él arguyó	él arguya	
nos'os argüimos	nos'os arguyamos	**Imperative-Don't**
vos'os argüisteis	vos'os arguyáis	no arguyas
ellos arguyeron	ellos arguyan	no arguya
		no arguyamos
Comp'nd tenses- 63-I-Haber +Past-P		no arguyáis
		no arguyan

23-O-Caer

Verb infinitive	Participles	Imperfect-subjunctive 1
Caer, to fall	caído: cayendo	yo cayera
		tú cayeras
Present	**Future**	él cayera
yo caigo	yo caeré	nos'os cayéramos
tú caes	tú caerás	vos'os cayerais
él cae	él caerá	ellos cayeran
nos'os caemos	nos'os caeremos	
vos'os caéis	vos'os caeréis	**Imp'fect-sub've 2**
ellos caen	ellos caerán	yo cayese
		tú cayeses
Imperfect	**Conditional**	él cayese
yo caía	yo caería	nos'os cayésemos
tú caías	tú caerías	vos'os cayeseis
él caía	él caería	ellos cayesen
nos'os caíamos	nos'os caeríamos	
vos'os caíais	vos'os caeríais	**Imperative-Do**
ellos caían	ellos caerían	(tú) cae
		(él) caiga
Preterite	**Present subj've**	(nos'os) caigamos
yo caí	yo caiga	(vos'os) caed
tú caíste	tú caigas	(ellos) caigan
él cayó	él caiga	
nos'os caímos	nos'os caigamos	**Imperative-Don't**
vos'os caísteis	vos'os caigáis	no caigas
ellos cayeron	ellos caigan	no caiga
		no caigamos
Comp'nd tenses- 63-I-Haber +Past-P		no caigáis
		no caigan

34

24(a)-S-Alentar

Verb infinitive	Participles	Imperfect-subjunctive 1
Alentar, to to encourage, to give heart to	alentado: alentando	yo alentara
		tú alentaras
Present	**Future**	él alentara
yo aliento	yo alentaré	nos'os alentáramos
tú alientas	tú alentarás	vos'os alentarais
él alienta	él alentará	ellos alentaran
nos'os alentamos	nos'os alentaremos	
vos'os alentáis	vos'os alentaréis	**Imp'fect-sub've 2**
ellos alientan	ellos alentarán	yo alentase
		tú alentases
Imperfect	**Conditional**	él alentase
yo alentaba	yo alentaría	nos'os alentásemos
tú alentabas	tú alentarías	vos'os alentaseis
él alentaba	él alentaría	ellos alentasen
nos'os alentábamos	nos'os alentaríamos	
vos'os alentabais	vos'os alentaríais	**Imperative-Do**
ellos alentaban	ellos alentarían	(tú) alienta
		(él) aliente
Preterite	**Present subj've**	(nos'os) alentemos
yo alenté	yo aliente	(vos'os) alentad
tú alentaste	tú alientes	(ellos) alienten
él alentó	él aliente	
nos'os alentamos	nos'os alentemos	**Imperative-Don't**
vos'os alentasteis	vos'os alentéis	no alientes
ellos alentaron	ellos alienten	no aliente
		no alentemos
Comp'nd tenses-63-I-Haber +Past-P		no alentéis
		no alienten

35

24(b)-S -Acertar

Verb infinitive	Participles	Imperfect-subjunctive 1
Acertar, to get right, to hit the target	acertado: acertando	yo acertara
		tú acertaras
Present	**Future**	él acertara
yo acierto	yo acertaré	nos'os acertáramos
tú aciertas	tú acertarás	vos'os acertarais
él acierta	él acertará	ellos acertaran
nos'os acertamos	nos'os acertaremos	
vos'os acertáis	vos'os acertaréis	**Imp'fect-sub've 2**
ellos aciertan	ellos acertarán	yo acertase
		tú acertases
Imperfect	**Conditional**	él acertase
yo acertaba	yo acertaría	nos'os acertásemos
tú acertabas	tú acertarías	vos'os acertaseis
él acertaba	él acertaría	ellos acertasen
nos'os acertábamos	nos'os acertaríamos	
vos'os acertabais	vos'os acertaríais	**Imperative-Do**
ellos acertaban	ellos acertarían	(tú) acierta
		(él) acierte
Preterite	**Present subj've**	(nos'os) acertemos
yo acerté	yo acierte	(vos'os) acertad
tú acertaste	tú aciertes	(ellos) acierten
él acertó	él acierte	
nos'os acertamos	nos'os acertemos	**Imperative-Don't**
vos'os acertasteis	vos'os acertéis	no aciertes
ellos acertaron	ellos acierten	no acierte
		no acertemos
Comp'nd tenses- 63-I-Haber +Past-P		no acertéis
		no acierten

36

25(a)-S-Perder

Verb infinitive	Participles	Imperfect-subjunctive 1
Perder, to lose	perdido: perdiendo	yo perdiera
		tú perdieras
Present	**Future**	él perdiera
yo pierdo	yo perderé	nos'os perdiéramos
tú pierdes	tú perderás	vos'os perdierais
él pierde	él perderá	ellos perdieran
nos'os perdemos	nos'os perderemos	
vos'os perdéis	vos'os perderéis	**Imp'fect-sub've 2**
ellos pierden	ellos perderán	yo perdiese
		tú perdieses
Imperfect	**Conditional**	él perdiese
yo perdía	yo perdería	nos'os perdiésemos
tú perdías	tú perderías	vos'os perdieseis
él perdía	él perdería	ellos perdiesen
nos'os perdíamos	nos'os perderíamos	
vos'os perdíais	vos'os perderíais	**Imperative-Do**
ellos perdían	ellos perderían	tú) pierde
		(él) pierda
Preterite	**Present subj've**	(nos'os) perdamos
yo perdí	yo pierda	(vos'os) perded
tú perdiste	tú pierdas	(ellos) pierdan
él perdió	él pierda	
nos'os perdimos	nos'os perdamos	**Imperative-Don't**
vos'os perdisteis	vos'os perdáis	no pierdas
ellos perdieron	ellos pierdan	no pierda
		no perdamos
Comp'nd tenses- 63-I-Haber +Past-P		no perdáis
		no pierdan

25(b)-S-Entender

Verb infinitive	Participles	Imperfect-subjunctive 1
Entender, to understand	entendido: entendiendo	yo entendiera
		tú entendieras
Present	**Future**	él entendiera
yo entiendo	yo entenderé	nos'os entendiéramos
tú entiendes	tú entenderás	vos'os entendierais
él entiende	él entenderá	ellos entendieran
nos'os entendemos	nos'os entenderemos	
vos'os entendéis	vos'os entenderéis	**Imp'fect-sub've 2**
ellos entienden	ellos entenderán	yo entendiese
		tú entendieses
Imperfect	**Conditional**	él entendiese
yo entendía	yo entendería	nos'os entendiésemos
tú entendías	tú entenderías	vos'os entendieseis
él entendía	él entendería	ellos entendiesen
nos'os entendíamos	nos'os entenderíamos	
vos'os entendíais	vos'os entenderíais	**Imperative-Do**
ellos entendían	ellos entenderían	(tú) entiende
		(él) entienda
Preterite	**Present subj've**	(nos'os) entendamos
yo entendí	yo entienda	(vos'os) entended
tú entendiste	tú entiendas	(ellos) entiendan
él entendió	él entienda	
nos'os entendimos	nos'os entendamos	**Imperative-Don't**
vos'os entendisteis	vos'os entendáis	no entiendas
ellos entendieron	ellos entiendan	no entienda
		no entendamos
Comp'nd tenses-63-I-Haber +Past-P		no entendáis
		no entiendan

26(a)-S-Aprobar

Verb infinitive	Participles	Imperfect-subjunctive 1
Aprobar, to approve, to consent to	aprobado: aprobando	yo aprobara
		tú aprobaras
Present	**Future**	él aprobara
yo apruebo	yo aprobaré	nos'os aprobáramos
tú apruebas	tú aprobarás	vos'os aprobarais
él aprueba	él aprobará	ellos aprobaran
nos'os aprobamos	nos'os aprobaremos	
vos'os aprobáis	vos'os aprobaréis	**Imp'fect-sub've 2**
ellos aprueban	ellos aprobarán	yo aprobase
		tú aprobases
Imperfect	**Conditional**	él aprobase
yo aprobaba	yo aprobaría	nos'os aprobásemos
tú aprobabas	tú aprobarías	vos'os aprobaseis
él aprobaba	él aprobaría	ellos aprobasen
nos'os aprobábamos	nos'os aprobaríamos	
vos'os aprobabais	vos'os aprobaríais	**Imperative-Do**
ellos aprobaban	ellos aprobarían	(tú) aprueba
		(él) apruebe
Preterite	**Present subj've**	(nos'os) aprobemos
yo aprobé	yo apruebe	(vos'os) aprobad
tú aprobaste	tú apruebes	(ellos) aprueben
él aprobó	él apruebe	
nos'os aprobamos	nos'os aprobemos	**Imperative-Don't**
vos'os aprobasteis	vos'os aprobéis	no apruebes
ellos aprobaron	ellos aprueben	no apruebe
		no aprobemos
Comp'nd tenses- 63-I-Haber +Past-P		no aprobéis
		no aprueben

39

26(b)-S-Acortar

Verb infinitive	Participles	Imperfect-subjunctive 1
Acortar, to shorten, to reduce	acortado: acortando	yo acortara
		tú acortaras
Present	**Future**	él acortara
yo acuerto	yo acortaré	nos'os acortáramos
tú acuertas	tú acortarás	vos'os acortarais
él acuerta	él acortará	ellos acortaran
nos'os acortamos	nos'os acortaremos	
vos'os acortáis	vos'os acortaréis	**Imp'fect-sub've 2**
ellos acuertan	ellos acortarán	yo acortase
		tú acortases
Imperfect	**Conditional**	él acortase
yo acortaba	yo acortaría	nos'os acortásemos
tú acortabas	tú acortarías	vos'os acortaseis
él acortaba	él acortaría	ellos acortasen
nos'os acortábamos	nos'os acortaríamos	
vos'os acortabais	vos'os acortaríais	**Imperative-Do**
ellos acortaban	ellos acortarían	(tú) acuerta
		(él) acuerte
Preterite	**Present subj've**	(nos'os) acortemos
yo acorté	yo acuerte	(vos'os) acortad
tú acortaste	tú acuertes	(ellos) acuerten
él acortó	él acuerte	
nos'os acortamos	nos'os acortemos	**Imperative-Don't**
vos'os acortasteis	vos'os acortéis	no acuertes
ellos acortaron	ellos acuerten	no acuerte
		no acortemos
Comp'nd tenses- 63-I-Haber +Past-P		no acortéis
		no acuerten

27(a)-S-Morder

Verb infinitive	Participles	Imperfect-subjunctive 1
Morder, to bite	mordido: mordiendo	yo mordiera
		tú mordieras
Present	**Future**	él mordiera
yo muerdo	yo morderé	nos'os mordiéramos
tú muerdes	tú morderás	vos'os mordierais
él muerde	él morderá	ellos mordieran
nos'os mordemos	nos'os morderemos	
vos'os mordéis	vos'os morderéis	**Imp'fect-sub've 2**
ellos muerden	ellos morderán	yo mordiese
		tú mordieses
Imperfect	**Conditional**	él mordiese
yo mordía	yo mordería	nos'os mordiésemos
tú mordías	tú morderías	vos'os mordieseis
él mordía	él mordería	ellos mordiesen
nos'os mordíamos	nos'os morderíamos	
vos'os mordíais	vos'os morderíais	**Imperative-Do**
ellos mordían	ellos morderían	(tú) muerde
		(él) muerda
Preterite	**Present subj've**	(nos'os) mordamos
yo mordí	yo muerda	(vos'os) morded
tú mordiste	tú muerdas	(ellos) muerdan
él mordió	él muerda	
nos'os mordimos	nos'os mordamos	**Imperative-Don't**
vos'os mordisteis	vos'os mordáis	no muerdas
ellos mordieron	ellos muerdan	no muerda
		no mordamos
Comp'nd tenses- 63-I-Haber +Past-P		no mordáis
		no muerdan

41

27(b)-S-Remover

Verb infinitive	Participles	Imperfect-subjunctive 1
Remover, to stir, to turn over	removido: removiendo	yo removiera
		tú removieras
Present	**Future**	él removiera
yo remuevo	yo removeré	nos'os removiéramos
tú remueves	tú removerás	vos'os removierais
él remueve	él removerá	ellos removieran
nos'os removemos	nos'os removeremos	
vos'os removéis	vos'os removeréis	**Imp'fect-sub've 2**
ellos remueven	ellos removerán	yo removiese
		tú removieses
Imperfect	**Conditional**	él removiese
yo removía	yo removería	nos'os removiésemos
tú removías	tú removerías	vos'os removieseis
él removía	él removería	ellos removiesen
nos'os removíamos	nos'os removeríamos	
vos'os removíais	vos'os removeríais	**Imperative-Do**
ellos removían	ellos removerían	(tú) remueve
		(él) remueva
Preterite	**Present subj've**	(nos'os) removamos
yo removí	yo remueva	(vos'os) removed
tú removiste	tú remuevas	(ellos) remuevan
él removió	él remueva	
nos'os removimos	nos'os removamos	**Imperative-Don't**
vos'os removisteis	vos'os remováis	no remuevas
ellos removieron	ellos remuevan	no remueva
		no removamos
Comp'nd tenses-63-I-Haber +Past-P		no remováis
		no remuevan

42

28-S-Oler

Verb infinitive	Participles	Imperfect-subjunctive 1
Oler, to smell.	olido: oliendo	yo oliera
		tú olieras
Present	**Future**	él oliera
yo huelo	yo oleré	nos'os oliéramos
tú hueles	tú olerás	vos'os olierais
él huele	él olerá	ellos olieran
nos'os olemos	nos'os oleremos	
vos'os oléis	vos'os oleréis	**Imp'fect-sub've 2**
ellos huelen	ellos olerán	yo oliese
		tú olieses
Imperfect	**Conditional**	él oliese
yo olía	yo olería	nos'os oliésemos
tú olías	tú olerías	vos'os olieseis
él olía	él olería	ellos oliesen
nos'os olíamos	nos'os oleríamos	
vos'os olíais	vos'os oleríais	**Imperative-Do**
ellos olían	ellos olerían	(tú) huele
		(él) huela
Preterite	**Present subj've**	(nos'os) olamos
yo olí	yo huela	(vos'os) oled
tú oliste	tú huelas	(ellos) huelan
él olió	él huela	
nos'os olimos	nos'os olamos	**Imperative-Don't**
vos'os olisteis	vos'os oláis	no huelas
ellos olieron	ellos huelan	no huela
		no olamos
Comp'nd tenses- 63-I-Haber +Past-P		no oláis
		no huelan

43

29(a)-S-Discernir

Verb infinitive	Participles	Imperfect-subjunctive 1
Discernir, to discern	discernido: discerniendo	yo discerniera
		tú discernieras
Present	**Future**	él discerniera
yo discierno	yo discerniré	nos'os discerniéramos
tú disciernes	tú discernirás	vos'os discernierais
él discierne	él discernirá	ellos discernieran
nos'os discernimos	nos'os discerniremos	
vos'os discernís	vos'os discerniréis	**Imp'fect-sub've 2**
ellos disciernen	ellos discernirán	yo discerniese
		tú discernieses
Imperfect	**Conditional**	él discerniese
yo discernía	yo discerniría	nos'os discerniésemos
tú discernías	tú discernirías	vos'os discernieseis
él discernía	él discerniría	ellos discerniesen
nos'os discerníamos	nos'os discerniríamos	
vos'os discerníais	vos'os discerniríais	**Imperative-Do**
ellos discernían	ellos discernirían	(tú) discierne
		(él) discierna
Preterite	**Present subj've**	(nos'os) discernamos
yo discerní	yo discierna	(vos'os) discernid
tú discerniste	tú disciernas	(ellos) disciernan
él discernió	él discierna	
nos'os discernimos	nos'os discernamos	**Imperative-Don't**
vos'os discernisteis	vos'os discernáis	no disciernas
ellos discernieron	ellos disciernan	no discierna
		no discernamos
Comp'nd tenses- 63-I-Haber +Past-P		no discernáis
		no disciernan

44

29(b)-S-Cernir

Verb infinitive	Participles	Imperfect-subjunctive 1
Cernir, to sift, to sieve	cernido: cerniendo	yo cerniera
		tú cernieras
Present	**Future**	él cerniera
yo cierno	yo cerniré	nos'os cerniéramos
tú ciernes	tú cernirás	vos'os cernierais
él cierne	él cernirá	ellos cernieran
nos'os cernimos	nos'os cerniremos	
vos'os cernís	vos'os cerniréis	**Imp'fect-sub've 2**
ellos ciernen	ellos cernirán	yo cerniese
		tú cernieses
Imperfect	**Conditional**	él cerniese
yo cernía	yo cerniría	nos'os cerniésemos
tú cernías	tú cernirías	vos'os cernieseis
él cernía	él cerniría	ellos cerniesen
nos'os cerníamos	nos'os cerniríamos	
vos'os cerníais	vos'os cerniríais	**Imperative-Do**
ellos cernían	ellos cernirían	(tú) cierne
		(él) cierna
Preterite	**Present subj've**	(nos'os) cernamos
yo cerní	yo cierna	(vos'os) cernid
tú cerniste	tú ciernas	(ellos) ciernan
él cernió	él cierna	
nos'os cernimos	nos'os cernamos	**Imperative-Don't**
vos'os cernisteis	vos'os cernáis	no ciernas
ellos cernieron	ellos ciernan	no cierna
		no cernamos
Comp'nd tenses- 63-I-Haber +Past-P		no cernáis
		no ciernan

45

30(a)-S-Sentir

Verb infinitive	Participles	Imperfect-subjunctive 1
Sentir, to feel	sentido: sintiendo	yo sintiera
		tú sintieras
Present	**Future**	él sintiera
yo siento	yo sentiré	nos'os sintiéramos
tú sientes	tú sentirás	vos'os sintierais
él siente	él sentirá	ellos sintieran
nos'os sentimos	nos'os sentiremos	
vos'os sentís	vos'os sentiréis	**Imp'fect-sub've 2**
ellos sienten	ellos sentirán	yo sintiese
		tú sintieses
Imperfect	**Conditional**	él sintiese
yo sentía	yo sentiría	nos'os sintiésemos
tú sentías	tú sentirías	vos'os sintieseis
él sentía	él sentiría	ellos sintiesen
nos'os sentíamos	nos'os sentiríamos	
vos'os sentíais	vos'os sentiríais	**Imperative-Do**
ellos sentían	ellos sentirían	(tú) siente
		(él) sienta
Preterite	**Present subj've**	(nos'os) sintamos
yo sentí	yo sienta	(vos'os) sentid
tú sentiste	tú sientas	(ellos) sientan
él sintió	él sienta	
nos'os sentimos	nos'os sintamos	**Imperative-Don't**
vos'os sentisteis	vos'os sintáis	no sientas
ellos sintieron	ellos sientan	no sienta
		no sintamos
Comp'nd tenses-63-I-Haber +Past-P		no sintáis
		no sientan

30(b)-S-Advertir

Verb infinitive	Participles	Imperfect-subjunctive 1
Advertir, to give notice, to give warning	advertido: advirtiendo	yo advirtiera
		tú advirtieras
Present	**Future**	él advirtiera
yo advierto	yo advertiré	nos'os advirtiéramos
tú adviertes	tú advertirás	vos'os advirtierais
él advierte	él advertirá	ellos advirtieran
nos'os advertimos	nos'os advertiremos	
vos'os advertís	vos'os advertiréis	**Imp'fect-sub've 2**
ellos advierten	ellos advertirán	yo advirtiese
		tú advirtieses
Imperfect	**Conditional**	él advirtiese
yo advertía	yo advertiría	nos'os advirtiésemos
tú advertías	tú advertirías	vos'os advirtieseis
él advertía	él advertiría	ellos advirtiesen
nos'os advertíamos	nos'os advertiríamos	
vos'os advertíais	vos'os advertiríais	**Imperative-Do**
ellos advertían	ellos advertirían	(tú) advierte
		(él) advierta
Preterite	**Present subj've**	(nos'os) advirtamos
yo advertí	yo advierta	(vos'os) advertid
tú advertiste	tú adviertas	(ellos) adviertan
él advirtió	él advierta	
nos'os advertimos	nos'os advirtamos	**Imperative-Don't**
vos'os advertisteis	vos'os advirtáis	no adviertas
ellos advirtieron	ellos adviertan	no advierta
		no advirtamos
Comp'nd tenses- 63-I-Haber +Past-P		no advirtáis
		no adviertan

31(a)-S-Servir

Verb infinitive	Participles	Imperfect-subjunctive 1
Servir, to serve	servido: sirviendo	yo sirviera
		tú sirvieras
Present	**Future**	él sirviera
yo sirvo	yo serviré	nos'os sirviéramos
tú sirves	tú servirás	vos'os sirvierais
él sirve	él servirá	ellos sirvieran
nos'os servimos	nos'os serviremos	
vos'os servís	vos'os serviréis	**Imp'fect-sub've 2**
ellos sirven	ellos servirán	yo sirviese
		tú sirvieses
Imperfect	**Conditional**	él sirviese
yo servía	yo serviría	nos'os sirviésemos
tú servías	tú servirías	vos'os sirvieseis
él servía	él serviría	ellos sirviesen
nos'os servíamos	nos'os serviríamos	
vos'os servíais	vos'os serviríais	**Imperative-Do**
ellos servían	ellos servirían	(tú) sirve
		(él) sirva
Preterite	**Present subj've**	(nos'os) sirvamos
yo serví	yo sirva	(vos'os) servid
tú serviste	tú sirvas	(ellos) sirvan
él sirvió	él sirva	
nos'os servimos	nos'os sirvamos	**Imperative-Don't**
vos'os servisteis	vos'os sirváis	no sirvas
ellos sirvieron	ellos sirvan	no sirva
		no sirvamos
Comp'nd tenses-63-I-Haber +Past-P		no sirváis
		no sirvan

31(b)-S-Competir

Verb infinitive	Participles	Imperfect-subjunctive 1
Competir, to compete	competido: compitiendo	yo compitiera
		tú compitieras
Present	**Future**	él compitiera
yo compito	yo competiré	nos'os compitiéramos
tú compites	tú competirás	vos'os compitierais
él compite	él competirá	ellos compitieran
nos'os competimos	nos'os competiremos	
vos'os competís	vos'os competiréis	**Imp'fect-sub've 2**
ellos compiten	ellos competirán	yo compitiese
		tú compitieses
Imperfect	**Conditional**	él compitiese
yo competía	yo competiría	nos'os compitiésemos
tú competías	tú competirías	vos'os compitieseis
él competía	él competiría	ellos compitiesen
nos'os competíamos	nos'os competiríamos	
vos'os competíais	vos'os competiríais	**Imperative-Do**
ellos competían	ellos competirían	(tú) compite
		(él) compita
Preterite	**Present subj've**	(nos'os) compitamos
yo competí	yo compita	(vos'os) competid
tú competiste	tú compitas	(ellos) compitan
él compitió	él compita	
nos'os competimos	nos'os compitamos	**Imperative-Don't**
vos'os competisteis	vos'os compitáis	no compitas
ellos compitieron	ellos compitan	no compita
		no compitamos
Comp'nd tenses- 63-I-Haber +Past-P		no compitáis
		no compitan

49

32(a)-S-Adquirir

Verb infinitive	Participles	Imperfect-subjunctive 1
Adquirir, to acquire	adquirido: adquiriendo	yo adquiriera
		tú adquirieras
Present	**Future**	él adquiriera
yo adquiero	yo adquiriré	nos'os adquiriéramos
tú adquieres	tú adquirirás	vos'os adquirierais
él adquiere	él adquirirá	ellos adquirieran
nos'os adquirimos	nos'os adquiriremos	
vos'os adquirís	vos'os adquiriréis	**Imp'fect-sub've 2**
ellos adquieren	ellos adquirirán	yo adquiriese
		tú adquirieses
Imperfect	**Conditional**	él adquiriese
yo adquiría	yo adquiriría	nos'os adquiriésemos
tú adquirías	tú adquirirías	vos'os adquirieseis
él adquiría	él adquiriría	ellos adquiriesen
nos'os adquiríamos	nos'os adquiriríamos	
vos'os adquiríais	vos'os adquiriríais	**Imperative-Do**
ellos adquirían	ellos adquirirían	(tú) adquiere
		(él) adquiera
Preterite	**Present subj've**	(nos'os) adquiramos
yo adquirí	yo adquiera	(vos'os) adquirid
tú adquiriste	tú adquieras	(ellos) adquieran
él adquirió	él adquiera	
nos'os adquirimos	nos'os adquiramos	**Imperative-Don't**
vos'os adquiristeis	vos'os adquiráis	no adquieras
ellos adquirieron	ellos adquieran	no adquiera
		no adquiramos
Comp'nd tenses- 63-I-Haber +Past-P		no adquiráis
		no adquieran

50

32(b)-S-Inquirir

Verb infinitive	Participles	Imperfect-subjunctive 1
Inquirir, to enquire, to investigate	inquirido: inquiriendo	yo inquiriera
		tú inquirieras
Present	**Future**	él inquiriera
yo inquiero	yo inquiriré	nos'os inquiriéramos
tú inquieres	tú inquirirás	vos'os inquirierais
él inquiere	él inquirirá	ellos inquirieran
nos'os inquirimos	nos'os inquiriremos	
vos'os inquirís	vos'os inquiriréis	**Imp'fect-sub've 2**
ellos inquieren	ellos inquirirán	yo inquiriese
		tú inquirieses
Imperfect	**Conditional**	él inquiriese
yo inquiría	yo inquiriría	nos'os inquiriésemos
tú inquirías	tú inquirirías	vos'os inquirieseis
él inquiría	él inquiriría	ellos inquiriesen
nos'os inquiríamos	nos'os inquiriríamos	
vos'os inquiríais	vos'os inquiriríais	**Imperative-Do**
ellos inquirían	ellos inquirirían	(tú) inquiere
		(él) inquiera
Preterite	**Present subj've**	(nos'os) inquiramos
yo inquirí	yo inquiera	(vos'os) inquirid
tú inquiriste	tú inquieras	(ellos) inquieran
él inquirió	él inquiera	
nos'os inquirimos	nos'os inquiramos	**Imperative-Don't**
vos'os inquiristeis	vos'os inquiráis	no inquieras
ellos inquirieron	ellos inquieran	no inquiera
		no inquiramos
Comp'nd tenses- 63-I-Haber +Past-P		no inquiráis
		no inquieran

51

33(a)-S-Dormir

Verb infinitive	Participles	Imperfect-subjunctive 1
Dormir, to sleep	dormido: durmiendo	yo durmiera
		tú durmieras
Present	**Future**	él durmiera
yo duermo	yo dormiré	nos'os durmiéramos
tú duermes	tú dormirás	vos'os durmierais
él duerme	él dormirá	ellos durmieran
nos'os dormimos	nos'os dormiremos	
vos'os dormís	vos'os dormiréis	**Imp'fect-sub've 2**
ellos duermen	ellos dormirán	yo durmiese
		tú durmieses
Imperfect	**Conditional**	él durmiese
yo dormía	yo dormiría	nos'os durmiésemos
tú dormías	tú dormirías	vos'os durmieseis
él dormía	él dormiría	ellos durmiesen
nos'os dormíamos	nos'os dormiríamos	
vos'os dormíais	vos'os dormiríais	**Imperative-Do**
ellos dormían	ellos dormirían	(tú) duerme
		(él) duerma
Preterite	**Present subj've**	(nos'os) durmamos
yo dormí	yo duerma	(vos'os) dormid
tú dormiste	tú duermas	(ellos) duerman
él durmió	él duerma	
nos'os dormimos	nos'os durmamos	**Imperative-Don't**
vos'os dormisteis	vos'os durmáis	no duermas
ellos durmieron	ellos duerman	no duerma
		no durmamos
Comp'nd tenses- 63-I-Haber +Past-P		no durmáis
		no duerman

33(b)-S-Morir

Verb infinitive	Participles	Imperfect-subjunctive 1
Morir, to die	muerto: muriendo	yo muriera
		tú murieras
Present	**Future**	él muriera
yo muero	yo moriré	nos'os muriéramos
tú mueres	tú morirás	vos'os murierais
él muere	él morirá	ellos murieran
nos'os morimos	nos'os moriremos	
vos'os morís	vos'os moriréis	**Imp'fect-sub've 2**
ellos mueren	ellos morirán	yo muriese
		tú murieses
Imperfect	**Conditional**	él muriese
yo moría	yo moriría	nos'os muriésemos
tú morías	tú morirías	vos'os murieseis
él moría	él moriría	ellos muriesen
nos'os moríamos	nos'os moriríamos	
vos'os moríais	vos'os moriríais	**Imperative-Do**
ellos morían	ellos morirían	(tú) muere
		(él) muera
Preterite	**Present subj've**	(nos'os) muramos
yo morí	yo muera	(vos'os) morid
tú moriste	tú mueras	(ellos) mueran
él murió	él muera	
nos'os morimos	nos'os muramos	**Imperative-Don't**
vos'os moristeis	vos'os muráis	no mueras
ellos murieron	ellos mueran	no muera
		no muramos
Comp'nd tenses- 63-I-Haber +Past-P		no muráis
		no mueran

34-S-Jugar

Verb infinitive	Participles	Imperfect-subjunctive 1
Jugar, to	jugado: jugando	yo jugara
		tú jugaras
Present	**Future**	él jugara
yo juego	yo jugaré	nos'os jugáramos
tú juegas	tú jugarás	vos'os jugarais
él juega	él jugará	ellos jugaran
nos'os jugamos	nos'os jugaremos	
vos'os jugáis	vos'os jugaréis	**Imp'fect-sub've 2**
ellos juegan	ellos jugarán	yo jugase
		tú jugases
Imperfect	**Conditional**	él jugase
yo jugaba	yo jugaría	nos'os jugásemos
tú jugabas	tú jugarías	vos'os jugaseis
él jugaba	él jugaría	ellos jugasen
nos'os jugábamos	nos'os jugaríamos	
vos'os jugabais	vos'os jugaríais	**Imperative-Do**
ellos jugaban	ellos jugarían	(tú) juega
		(él) juegue
Preterite	**Present subj've**	(nos'os) juguemos
yo jugué	yo juegue	(vos'os) jugad
tú jugaste	tú juegues	(ellos) jueguen
él jugó	él juegue	
nos'os jugamos	nos'os juguemos	**Imperative-Don't**
vos'os jugasteis	vos'os juguéis	no juegues
ellos jugaron	ellos jueguen	no juegue
		no juguemos
Comp'nd tenses- 63-I-Haber +Past-P		no juguéis
		no jueguen

35(a)-S-Reír

Verb infinitive	Participles	Imperfect-subjunctive 1
Reír, to laugh	reído: riendo	yo riera
		tú rieras
Present	**Future**	él riera
yo río	yo reiré	nos'os riéramos
tú ríes	tú reirás	vos'os rierais
él ríe	él reirá	ellos rieran
nos'os reímos	nos'os reiremos	
vos'os reís	vos'os reiréis	**Imp'fect-sub've 2**
ellos ríen	ellos reirán	yo riese
		tú rieses
Imperfect	**Conditional**	él riese
yo reía	yo reiría	nos'os riésemos
tú reías	tú reirías	vos'os rieseis
él reía	él reiría	ellos riesen
nos'os reíamos	nos'os reiríamos	
vos'os reíais	vos'os reiríais	**Imperative-Do**
ellos reían	ellos reirían	(tú) ríe
		(él) ría
Preterite	**Present subj've**	(nos'os) riamos
yo reí	yo ría	(vos'os) reíd
tú reíste	tú rías	(ellos) rían
él rió	él ría	
nos'os reímos	nos'os riamos	**Imperative-Don't**
vos'os reísteis	vos'os riáis	no rías
ellos rieron	ellos rían	no ría
		no riamos
Comp'nd tenses- 63-I-Haber +Past-P		no riáis
		no rían

35(b)-S-Freír

Verb infinitive	Participles	Imperfect-subjunctive 1
Freír, to fry	freído; frito: friendo	yo friera
		tú frieras
Present	**Future**	él friera
yo frío	yo freiré	nos'os friéramos
tú fríes	tú freirás	vos'os frierais
él fríe	él freirá	ellos frieran
nos'os freímos	nos'os freiremos	
vos'os freís	vos'os freiréis	**Imp'fect-sub've 2**
ellos fríen	ellos freirán	yo friese
		tú frieses
Imperfect	**Conditional**	él friese
yo freía	yo freiría	nos'os friésemos
tú freías	tú freirías	vos'os frieseis
él freía	él freiría	ellos friesen
nos'os freíamos	nos'os freiríamos	
vos'os freíais	vos'os freiríais	**Imperative-Do**
ellos freían	ellos freirían	(tú) fríe
		(él) fría
Preterite	**Present subj've**	(nos'os) friamos
yo freí	yo fría	(vos'os) freíd
tú freíste	tú frías	(ellos) frían
él frió	él fría	
nos'os freímos	nos'os friamos	**Imperative-Don't**
vos'os freísteis	vos'os friáis	no frías
ellos frieron	ellos frían	no fría
		no friamos
Comp'nd tenses- 63-I-Haber +Past-P		no friáis
		no frían

56

36(a)-S-Colegir

Verb infinitive	Participles	Imperfect-subjunctive 1
Colegir, to gather	colegido: coligiendo	yo coligiera
		tú coligieras
Present	**Future**	él coligiera
yo colijo	yo colegiré	nos'os coligiéramos
tú coliges	tú colegirás	vos'os coligierais
él colige	él colegirá	ellos coligieran
nos'os colegimos	nos'os colegiremos	
vos'os colegís	vos'os colegiréis	**Imp'fect-sub've 2**
ellos coligen	ellos colegirán	yo coligiese
		tú coligieses
Imperfect	**Conditional**	él coligiese
yo colegía	yo colegiría	nos'os coligiésemos
tú colegías	tú colegirías	vos'os coligieseis
él colegía	él colegiría	ellos coligiesen
nos'os colegíamos	nos'os colegiríamos	
vos'os colegíais	vos'os colegiríais	**Imperative-Do**
ellos colegían	ellos colegirían	(tú) colige
		(él) colija
Preterite	**Present subj've**	(nos'os) colijamos
yo colegí	yo colija	(vos'os) colegid
tú colegiste	tú colijas	(ellos) colijan
él coligió	él colija	
nos'os colegimos	nos'os colijamos	**Imperative-Don't**
vos'os colegisteis	vos'os colijáis	no colijas
ellos coligieron	ellos colijan	no colija
		no colijamos
Comp'nd tenses- 63-I-Haber +Past-P		no colijáis
		no colijan

57

36(b)-S-Elegir

Verb infinitive	Participles	Imperfect-subjunctive 1
Elegir, to select, to choose	elegido: eligiendo	yo eligiera
		tú eligieras
Present	**Future**	él eligiera
yo elijo	yo elegiré	nos'os eligiéramos
tú eliges	tú elegirás	vos'os eligierais
él elige	él elegirá	ellos eligieran
nos'os elegimos	nos'os elegiremos	
vos'os elegís	vos'os elegiréis	**Imp'fect-sub've 2**
ellos eligen	ellos elegirán	yo eligiese
		tú eligieses
Imperfect	**Conditional**	él eligiese
yo elegía	yo elegiría	nos'os eligiésemos
tú elegías	tú elegirías	vos'os eligieseis
él elegía	él elegiría	ellos eligiesen
nos'os elegíamos	nos'os elegiríamos	
vos'os elegíais	vos'os elegiríais	**Imperative-Do**
ellos elegían	ellos elegirían	(tú) elige
		(él) elija
Preterite	**Present subj've**	(nos'os) elijamos
yo elegí	yo elija	(vos'os) elegid
tú elegiste	tú elijas	(ellos) elijan
él eligió	él elija	
nos'os elegimos	nos'os elijamos	**Imperative-Don't**
vos'os elegisteis	vos'os elijáis	no elijas
ellos eligieron	ellos elijan	no elija
		no elijamos
Comp'nd tenses-63-I-Haber +Past-P		no elijáis
		no elijan

37-R-RF-Abrirse   Note: participles.

Verb infinitive	Participles	Imperfect-subjunctive 1
Abrirse, to open our	abierto: abriéndose	me abriera
		te abrieras
Present	**Future**	se abriera
me abro	me abriré	nos abriéramos
te abres	te abrirás	os abrierais
se abre	se abrirá	se abrieran
nos abrimos	nos abriremos	
os abrís	os abriréis	**Imp'fect-sub've 2**
se abren	se abrirán	me abriese
		te abrieses
Imperfect	**Conditional**	se abriese
me abría	me abriría	nos abriésemos
te abrías	te abrirías	os abrieseis
se abría	se abriría	se abriesen
nos abríamos	nos abriríamos	
os abríais	os abriríais	**Imperative-Do**
se abrían	se abrirían	(tú) ábrete
		(él) ábrase
Preterite	**Present subj've**	(nos'os) abrámonos
me abrí	me abra	(vos'os) abríos
te abriste	te abras	(ellos) ábranse
se abrió	se abra	
nos abrimos	nos abramos	**Imperative-Don't**
os abristeis	os abráis	no te abras
se abrieron	se abran	no se abra
		no nos abramos
Comp'nd tenses-63-I-Haber +Past-P		no os abráis
		no se abran

59

38-R-RF-Alejarse

Verb infinitive	Participles	Imperfect-subjunctive 1
Alejarse, to draw further off	alejado: alejándose	me alejara
		te alejaras
Present	**Future**	se alejara
me alejo	me alejaré	nos alejáramos
te alejas	te alejarás	os alejarais
se aleja	se alejará	se alejaran
nos alejamos	nos alejaremos	
os alejáis	os alejaréis	**Imp'fect-sub've 2**
se alejan	se alejarán	me alejase
		te alejases
Imperfect	**Conditional**	se alejase
me alejaba	me alejaría	nos alejásemos
te alejabas	te alejarías	os alejaseis
se alejaba	se alejaría	se alejasen
nos alejábamos	nos alejaríamos	
os alejabais	os alejaríais	**Imperative-Do**
se alejaban	se alejarían	(tú) aléjate
		(él) aléjese
Preterite	**Present subj've**	(nos'os) alejémonos
me alejé	me aleje	(vos'os) alejaos
te alejaste	te alejes	(ellos) aléjense
se alejó	se aleje	
nos alejamos	nos alejemos	**Imperative-Don't**
os alejasteis	os alejéis	no te alejes
se alejaron	se alejen	no se aleje
		no nos alejemos
Comp'nd tenses- 63-I-Haber +Past-P		no os alejéis
		no se alejen

39-I-RF-Caerse

Note: participles. present. preterite. present subjunctive. imperfect-subjunctive. imperative.

Verb infinitive	Participles	Imperfect-subjunctive 1
Caerse, to fall down	caído: cayéndose	me cayera
		te cayeras
Present	**Future**	se cayera
me caigo	me cacré	nos cayéramos
te caes	te caerás	os cayerais
se cae	se caerá	se cayeran
nos caemos	nos caeremos	
os caéis	os caeréis	**Imp'fect-sub've 2**
se caen	se caerán	me cayese
		te cayeses
Imperfect	**Conditional**	se cayese
me caía	me caería	nos cayésemos
te caías	te caerías	os cayeseis
se caía	se caería	se cayesen
nos caíamos	nos caeríamos	
os caíais	os caeríais	**Imperative-Do**
se caían	se caerían	(tú) cáete
		(él) cáigase
Preterite	**Present subj've**	(nos'os) caigámonos
me caí	me caiga	(vos'os) caeos
te caíste	te caigas	(ellos) cáiganse
se cayó	se caiga	
nos caímos	nos caigamos	**Imperative-Don't**
os caísteis	os caigáis	no te caigas
se cayeron	se caigan	no se caiga
		no nos caigamos
Comp'nd tenses- 63-I-Haber +Past-P		no os caigáis
		no se caigan

40-I-RF-Convertirse

Note: participles. present. preterite. present subjunctive. imperfect-subjunctive. imperative.

Verb infinitive	Participles	Imperfect-subjunctive 1
Convertirse, to be transformed, to be converted	convertido: convirtiéndose	me convirtiera
		te convirtieras
Present	**Future**	se convirtiera
me convierto	me convertiré	nos convirtiéramos
te conviertes	te convertirás	os convirtierais
se convierte	se convertirá	se convirtieran
nos convertimos	nos convertiremos	
os convertís	os convertiréis	**Imp'fect-sub've 2**
se convierten	se convertirán	me convirtiese
		te convirtieses
Imperfect	**Conditional**	se convirtiese
me convertía	me convertiría	nos convirtiésemos
te convertías	te convertirías	os convirtieseis
se convertía	se convertiría	se convirtiesen
nos convertíamos	nos convertiríamos	
os convertíais	os convertiríais	**Imperative-Do**
se convertían	se convertirían	(tú) conviértete
		(él) conviértase
Preterite	**Present subj've**	(nos'os) convirtámonos
me convertí	me convierta	(vos'os) convertíos
te convertiste	te conviertas	(ellos) conviértanse
se convirtió	se convierta	
nos convertimos	nos convirtamos	**Imperative-Don't**
os convertisteis	os convirtáis	no te conviertas
se convirtieron	se conviertan	no se convierta
		no nos convirtamos
Comp'nd tenses- 63-I-Haber +Past-P		no os convirtáis
		no se conviertan

62

41-S-RF-Defenderse

Note: present. present subjunctive. imperative.

Verb infinitive	Participles	Imperfect-subjunctive 1
Defenderse, to defend oneself	defendido: defendiéndose	me defendiera
		te defendieras
Present	**Future**	se defendiera
me defiendo	me defenderé	nos defendiéramos
te defiendes	te defenderás	os defendierais
se defiende	se defenderá	se defendieran
nos defendemos	nos defenderemos	
os defendéis	os defenderéis	**Imp'fect-sub've 2**
se defienden	se defenderán	me defendiese
		te defendieses
Imperfect	**Conditional**	se defendiese
me defendía	me defendería	nos defendiésemos
te defendías	te defenderías	os defendieseis
se defendía	se defendería	se defendiesen
nos defendíamos	nos defenderíamos	
os defendíais	os defenderíais	**Imperative-Do**
se defendían	se defenderían	(tú) defiéndete
		(él) defiéndase
Preterite	**Present subj've**	(nos'os) defendámonos
me defendí	me defienda	(vos'os) defendeos
te defendiste	te defiendas	(ellos) defiéndanse
se defendió	se defienda	
nos defendimos	nos defendamos	**Imperative-Don't**
os defendisteis	os defendáis	no te defiendas
se defendieron	se defiendan	no se defienda
		no nos defendamos
Comp'nd tenses-63-I-Haber +Past-P		no os defendáis
		no se defiendan

63

42-S-RF-Despedirse

Note: participles. present. preterite. present subjunctive. imperfect-subjunctive. imperative.

Verb infinitive	Participles	Imperfect-subjunctive 1
Despedirse, to say goodbye to	despedido: despidiéndose	me despidiera
		te despidieras
Present	**Future**	se despidiera
me despido	me despediré	nos despidiéramos
te despides	te despedirás	os despidierais
se despide	se despedirá	se despidieran
nos despedimos	nos despediremos	
os despedís	os despediréis	**Imp'fect-sub've 2**
se despiden	se despedirán	me despidiese
		te despidieses
Imperfect	**Conditional**	se despidiese
me despedía	me despediría	nos despidiésemos
te despedías	te despedirías	os despidieseis
se despedía	se despediría	se despidiesen
nos despedíamos	nos despediríamos	
os despedíais	os despediríais	**Imperative-Do**
se despedían	se despedirían	(tú) despídete
		(él) despídase
Preterite	**Present subj've**	(nos'os) despidámonos
me despedí	me despida	(vos'os) despedíos
te despediste	te despidas	(ellos) despídanse
se despidió	se despida	
nos despedimos	nos despidamos	**Imperative-Don't**
os despedisteis	os despidáis	no te despidas
se despidieron	se despidan	no se despida
		no nos despidamos
Comp'nd tenses-63-I-Haber +Past-P		no os despidáis
		no se despidan

64

43-I-RF-Desvestirse

Note: participles. present. preterite. present subjunctive. imperfect-subjunctive. imperative.

Verb infinitive	Participles	Imperfect-subjunctive 1
Desvestirse, to undress oneself	desvestido: desvistiéndose	me desvistiera
		te desvistieras
Present	**Future**	se desvistiera
me desvisto	me desvestiré	nos desvistiéramos
te desvistes	te desvestirás	os desvistierais
se desviste	se desvestirá	se desvistieran
nos desvestimos	nos desvestiremos	
os desvestís	os desvestiréis	**Imp'fect-sub've 2**
se desvisten	se desvestirán	me desvistiese
		te desvistieses
Imperfect	**Conditional**	se desvistiese
me desvestía	me desvestiría	nos desvistiésemos
te desvestías	te desvestirías	os desvistieseis
se desvestía	se desvestiría	se desvistiesen
nos desvestíamos	nos desvestiríamos	
os desvestíais	os desvestiríais	**Imperative-Do**
se desvestían	se desvestirían	(tú) desvístete
		(él) desvístase
Preterite	**Present subj've**	(nos'os) desvistámonos
me desvestí	me desvista	(vos'os) desvestíos
te desvestiste	te desvistas	(ellos) desvístanse
se desvistió	se desvista	
nos desvestimos	nos desvistamos	**Imperative-Don't**
os desvestisteis	os desvistáis	no te desvistas
se desvistieron	se desvistan	no se desvista
		no nos desvistamos
Comp'nd tenses- 63-I-Haber +Past-P		no os desvistáis
		no se desvistan

65

44-I-RF-Detenerse

Note: present. preterite. future. conditional. present subjunctive. imperfect-subjunctive. imperative.

Verb infinitive	Participles	Imperfect-subjunctive 1
Detenerse, to stop oneself	detenido: deteniéndose	me detuviera
		te detuvieras
Present	**Future**	se detuviera
me detengo	me detendré	nos detuviéramos
te detienes	te detendrás	os detuvierais
se detiene	se detendrá	se detuvieran
nos detenemos	nos detendremos	
os detenéis	os detendréis	**Imp'fect-sub've 2**
se detienen	se detendrán	me detuviese
		te detuvieses
Imperfect	**Conditional**	se detuviese
me detenía	me detendría	nos detuviésemos
te detenías	te detendrías	os detuvieseis
se detenía	se detendría	se detuviesen
nos deteníamos	nos detendríamos	
os deteníais	os detendríais	**Imperative-Do**
se detenían	se detendrían	(tú) detente
		(él) deténgase
Preterite	**Present subj've**	(nos'os) detengámonos
me detuve	me detenga	(vos'os) deteneos
te detuviste	te detengas	(ellos deténganse
se detuvo	se detenga	
nos detuvimos	nos detengamos	**Imperative-Don't**
os detuvisteis	os detengáis	no te detengas
se detuvieron	se detengan	no se detenga
		no nos detengamos
Comp'nd tenses- 63-I-Haber +Past-P		no os detengáis
		no se detengan

66

45-I-RF-Dirigirse

Note: participles. present. present subjunctive. imperative.

Verb infinitive	Participles	Imperfect-subjunctive 1
Dirigirse, to direct oneself, to make one's way	dirigido: dirigiéndose	me dirigiera
		te dirigieras
Present	**Future**	se dirigiera
me dirijo	me dirigiré	nos dirigiéramos
te diriges	te dirigirás	os dirigierais
se dirige	se dirigirá	se dirigieran
nos dirigimos	nos dirigiremos	
os dirigís	os dirigiréis	**Imp'fect-sub've 2**
se dirigen	se dirigirán	me dirigiese
		te dirigieses
Imperfect	**Conditional**	se dirigiese
me dirigía	me dirigiría	nos dirigiésemos
te dirigías	te dirigirías	os dirigieseis
se dirigía	se dirigiría	se dirigiesen
nos dirigíamos	nos dirigiríamos	
os dirigíais	os dirigiríais	**Imperative-Do**
se dirigían	se dirigirían	(tú) dirígete
		(él) diríjase
Preterite	**Present subj've**	(nos'os) dirijámonos
me dirigí	me dirija	(vos'os) dirigíos
te dirigiste	te dirijas	(ellos) diríjanse
se dirigió	se dirija	
nos dirigimos	nos dirijamos	**Imperative-Don't**
os dirigisteis	os dirijáis	no te dirijas
se dirigieron	se dirijan	no se dirija
		no nos dirijamos
Comp'nd tenses- 63-I-Haber +Past-P		no os dirijáis
		no se dirijan

67

46-I-RF-Divertirse

Note: participles. present. preterite. present subjunctive. imperfect-subjunctive. imperative.

Verb infinitive	Participles	Imperfect-subjunctive 1
Divertirse, to amuse oneself	divertido: divirtiéndose	me divirtiera
		te divirtieras
Present	**Future**	se divirtiera
me divierto	me divertiré	nos divirtiéramos
te diviertes	te divertirás	os divirtierais
se divierte	se divertirá	se divirtieran
nos divertimos	nos divertiremos	
os divertís	os divertiréis	**Imp'fect-sub've 2**
se divierten	se divertirán	me divirtiese
		te divirtieses
Imperfect	**Conditional**	se divirtiese
me divertía	me divertiría	nos divirtiésemos
te divertías	te divertirías	os divirtieseis
se divertía	se divertiría	se divirtiesen
nos divertíamos	nos divertiríamos	
os divertíais	os divertiríais	**Imperative-Do**
se divertían	se divertirían	(tú) diviértete
		(él) diviértase
Preterite	**Present subj've**	(nos'os) divirtámonos
me divertí	me divierta	(vos'os) divertíos
te divertiste	te diviertas	(ellos) diviértanse
se divirtió	se divierta	
nos divertimos	nos divirtamos	**Imperative-Don't**
os divertisteis	os divirtáis	no te diviertas
se divirtieron	se diviertan	no se divierta
		no nos divirtamos
Comp'nd tenses- 63-I-Haber +Past-P		no os divirtáis
		no se diviertan

47-R-RF-Inscribirse
Note: participles

Verb infinitive	Participles	Imperfect-subjunctive 1
Inscribirse, to sign up to	inscrito: inscribiéndose	me inscribiera
		te inscribieras
Present	**Future**	se inscribiera
me inscribo	me inscribiré	nos inscribiéramos
te inscribes	te inscribirás	os inscribierais
se inscribe	se inscribirá	se inscribieran
nos inscribimos	nos inscribiremos	
os inscribís	os inscribiréis	**Imp'fect-sub've 2**
se inscriben	se inscribirán	me inscribiese
		te inscribieses
Imperfect	**Conditional**	se inscribiese
me inscribía	me inscribiría	nos inscribiésemos
te inscribías	te inscribirías	os inscribieseis
se inscribía	se inscribiría	se inscribiesen
nos inscribíamos	nos inscribiríamos	
os inscribíais	os inscribiríais	**Imperative-Do**
se inscribían	se inscribirían	(tú) inscríbete
		(él) inscríbase
Preterite	**Present subj've**	(nos'os) inscribámonos
me inscribí	me inscriba	(vos'os) inscribíos
te inscribiste	te inscribas	(ellos) inscríbanse
se inscribió	se inscriba	
nos inscribimos	nos inscribamos	**Imperative-Don't**
os inscribisteis	os inscribáis	no te inscribas
se inscribieron	se inscriban	no se inscriba
		no nos inscribamos
Comp'nd tenses- 63-I-Haber +Past-P		no os inscribáis
		no se inscriban

48-I-RF-Irse

Note: participles. present. preterite. imperfect. present subjunctive. imperfect-subjunctive. imperative.

Verb infinitive	Participles	Imperfect-subjunctive 1
Irse, to go away	ido: yéndose	me fuera
		te fueras
Present	**Future**	se fuera
me voy	me iré	nos fuéramos
te vas	te irás	os fuerais
se va	se irá	se fueran
nos vamos	nos iremos	
os vais	os iréis	**Imp'fect-sub've 2**
se van	se irán	me fuese
		te fueses
Imperfect	**Conditional**	se fuese
me iba	me iría	nos fuésemos
te ibas	te irías	os fueseis
se iba	se iría	se fuesen
nos íbamos	nos iríamos	
os ibais	os iríais	**Imperative-Do**
se iban	se irían	(tú) vete
		(él) váyase
Preterite	**Present subj've**	(nos'os) vámonos
me fui	me vaya	(vos'os) idos
te fuiste	te vayas	(ellos) váyanse
se fue	se vaya	
nos fuimos	nos vayamos	**Imperative-Don't**
os fuisteis	os vayáis	no te vayas
se fueron	se vayan	no se vaya
		no nos vayamos
Comp'nd tenses- 63-I-Haber +Past-P		no os vayáis
		no se vayan

70

49-R-RF-Levantarse

Verb infinitive	Participles	Imperfect-subjunctive 1
Levantarse, to get up, to arise	levantado: levantándose	me levantara
		te levantaras
Present	me levantaré	se levantara
me levanto	te levantarás	nos levantáramos
te levantas	se levantará	os levantarais
se levanta	nos levantaremos	se levantaran
nos levantamos	os levantaréis	
os levantáis	se levantarán	**Imp'fect-sub've 2**
se levantan		me levantase
	Conditional	te levantases
Imperfect	me levantaría	se levantase
me levantaba	te levantarías	nos levantásemos
te levantabas	se levantaría	os levantaseis
se levantaba	nos levantaríamos	se levantasen
nos levantábamos	os levantaríais	
os levantabais	se levantarían	**Imperative-Do**
se levantaban		(tú) levántate
		(él) levántese
Preterite	**Present subj've**	(nos'os) levantémonos
me levanté	me levante	(vos'os) levantaos
te levantaste	te levantes	(ellos) levántense
se levantó	se levante	
nos levantamos	nos levantemos	**Imperative-Don't**
os levantasteis	os levantéis	no te levantes
se levantaron	se levanten	no se levante
		no nos levantemos
Comp'nd tenses-63-I-Haber +Past-P		no os levantéis
		no se levanten

71

50-I-RF-Morderse

Note: present. present subjunctive. imperative.

Verb infinitive	Participles	Imperfect-subjunctive 1
Morderse, to bite oneself	mordido: mordiéndose	me mordiera
		te mordieras
Present	**Future**	se mordiera
me muerdo	me morderé	nos mordiéramos
te muerdes	te morderás	os mordierais
se muerde	se morderá	se mordieran
nos mordemos	nos morderemos	
os mordéis	os morderéis	**Imp'fect-sub've 2**
se muerden	se morderán	me mordiese
		te mordieses
Imperfect	**Conditional**	se mordiese
me mordía	me mordería	nos mordiésemos
te mordías	te morderías	os mordieseis
se mordía	se mordería	se mordiesen
nos mordíamos	nos morderíamos	
os mordíais	os morderíais	**Imperative-Do**
se mordían	se morderían	((tú) muérdete
		(él) muérdase
Preterite	**Present subj've**	(nos'os) mordámonos
me mordí	me muerda	(vos'os) mordeos
te mordiste	te muerdas	(ellos) muérdanse
se mordió	se muerda	
nos mordimos	nos mordamos	**Imperative-Don't**
os mordisteis	os mordáis	no te muerdas
se mordieron	se muerdan	no se muerda
		no nos mordamos
Comp'nd tenses- 63-I-Haber +Past-P		no os mordáis
		no se muerdan

72

51-I-RF-Ponerse

Note: present. preterite. future. conditional. present subjunctive. imperfect-subjunctive. imperative.

Verb infinitive	Participles	Imperfect-subjunctive 1
Ponerse, to put on, to become	puesto: poniéndose	me pusiera
		te pusieras
Present	**Future**	se pusiera
me pongo	me pondré	nos pusiéramos
te pones	te pondrás	os pusierais
se pone	se pondrá	se pusieran
nos ponemos	nos pondremos	
os ponéis	os pondréis	**Imp'fect-sub've 2**
se ponen	se pondrán	me pusiese
		te pusieses
Imperfect	**Conditional**	se pusiese
me ponía	me pondría	nos pusiésemos
te ponías	te pondrías	os pusieseis
se ponía	se pondría	se pusiesen
nos poníamos	nos pondríamos	
os poníais	os pondríais	**Imperative-Do**
se ponían	se pondrían	(tú) ponte
		(él) póngase
Preterite	**Present subj've**	(nos'os) pongámonos
me puse	me ponga	(vos'os) poneos
te pusiste	te pongas	(ellos) pónganse
se puso	se ponga	
nos pusimos	nos pongamos	**Imperative-Don't**
os pusisteis	os pongáis	no te pongas
se pusieron	se pongan	no se ponga
		no nos pongamos
Comp'nd tenses- 63-I-Haber +Past-P		no os pongáis
		no se pongan

73

52-S-RF-Reírse

Note: participles. present. preterite. present subjunctive. imperfect-subjunctive. imperative.

Verb infinitive	Participles	Imperfect-subjunctive 1
Reírse, to laugh at	reído: riéndose	me riera
		te rieras
Present	**Future**	se riera
me río	me reiré	nos riéramos
te ríes	te reirás	os rierais
se ríe	se reirá	se rieran
nos reímos	nos reiremos	
os reís	os reiréis	**Imp'fect-sub've 2**
se ríen	se reirán	me riese
		te rieses
Imperfect	**Conditional**	se riese
me reía	me reiría	nos riésemos
te reías	te reirías	os rieseis
se reía	se reiría	se riesen
nos reíamos	nos reiríamos	
os reíais	os reiríais	**Imperative-Do**
se reían	se reirían	(tú) rìete
		(él) rìase
Preterite	**Present subj've**	(nos'os) riámonos
me reí	me ría	(vos'os) reíos
te reíste	te rías	(ellos) rìanse
se rió	se ría	
nos reímos	nos riamos	**Imperative-Don't**
os reísteis	os riáis	no te rías
se rieron	se rían	no se ría
		no nos riamos
Comp'nd tenses- 63-I-Haber +Past-P		no os riáis
		no se rían

53-I-RF-Sentarse
Note:. present. preterite. present subjunctive. imperative.

Verb infinitive	Participles	Imperfect-subjunctive 1
Sentarse, to sit down	sentado: sentándose	me sentara
		te sentaras
Present	**Future**	se sentara
me siento	me sentaré	nos sentáramos
te sientas	te sentarás	os sentarais
se sienta	se sentará	se sentaran
nos sentamos	nos sentaremos	
os sentáis	os sentaréis	**Imp'fect-sub've 2**
se sientan	se sentarán	me sentase
		te sentases
Imperfect	**Conditional**	se sentase
me sentaba	me sentaría	nos sentásemos
te sentabas	te sentarías	os sentaseis
se sentaba	se sentaría	se sentasen
nos sentábamos	nos sentaríamos	
os sentabais	os sentaríais	**Imperative-Do**
se sentaban	se sentarían	(tú) siéntate
		(él) siéntese
Preterite	**Present subj've**	(nos'os) sentémonos
me senté	me siente	(vos'os) sentaos
te sentaste	te sientes	(ellos) siéntense
se sentó	se siente	
nos sentamos	nos sentemos	**Imperative-Don't**
os sentasteis	os sentéis	no te sientes
se sentaron	se sienten	no se siente
		no nos sentemos
Comp'nd tenses- 63-I-Haber +Past-P		no os sentéis
		no se sienten

75

54-S-RF-Sentirse

Note: participles. present. preterite. present subjunctive. imperfect-subjunctive. imperative.

Verb infinitive	Participles	Imperfect-subjunctive 1
Sentirse, to feel	sentido: sintiéndose	me sintiera
		te sintieras
Present	**Future**	se sintiera
me siento	me sentiré	nos sintiéramos
te sientes	te sentirás	os sintierais
se siente	se sentirá	se sintieran
nos sentimos	nos sentiremos	
os sentís	os sentiréis	**Imp'fect-sub've 2**
se sienten	se sentirán	me sintiese
		te sintieses
Imperfect	**Conditional**	se sintiese
me sentía	me sentiría	nos sintiésemos
te sentías	te sentirías	os sintieseis
se sentía	se sentiría	se sintiesen
nos sentíamos	nos sentiríamos	
os sentíais	os sentiríais	**Imperative-Do**
se sentían	se sentirían	(tú) siéntete
		(él) siéntase
Preterite	**Present subj've**	(nos'os) sintámonos
me sentí	me sienta	(vos'os) sentíos
te sentiste	te sientas	(ellos) siéntanse
se sintió	se sienta	
nos sentimos	nos sintamos	**Imperative-Don't**
os sentisteis	os sintáis	no te sientas
se sintieron	se sientan	no se sienta
		no nos sintamos
Comp'nd tenses- 63-I-Haber +Past-P		no os sintáis
		no se sientan

55-I-Andar
Note: preterite. imperfect-subjunctive.

Verb infinitive	Participles	Imperfect-subjunctive 1
Andar, to walk	andado: andando	yo anduviera
		tú anduvieras
Present	**Future**	él anduviera
yo ando	yo andaré	nos'os anduviéramos
tú andas	tú andarás	vos'os anduvierais
él anda	él andará	ellos anduvieran
nos'os andamos	nos'os andaremos	
vos'os andáis	vos'os andaréis	**Imp'fect-sub've 2**
ellos andan	ellos andarán	yo anduviese
		tú anduvieses
Imperfect	**Conditional**	él anduviese
yo andaba	yo andaría	nos'os anduviésemos
tú andabas	tú andarías	vos'os anduvieseis
él andaba	él andaría	ellos anduviesen
nos'os andábamos	nos'os andaríamos	
vos'os andabais	vos'os andaríais	**Imperative-Do**
ellos andaban	ellos andarían	(tú) anda
		(él) ande
Preterite	**Present subj've**	(nos'os) andemos
yo anduve	yo ande	(vos'os) andad
tú anduviste	tú andes	(ellos) anden
él anduvo	él ande	
nos'os anduvimos	nos'os andemos	**Imperative-Don't**
vos'os anduvisteis	vos'os andéis	no andes
ellos anduvieron	ellos anden	no ande
		no andemos
Comp'nd tenses- 63-I-Haber +Past-P		no andéis
		no anden

56-I-Asir

Note: present. preterite. present subjunctive. imperative.

Verb infinitive	Participles	Imperfect-subjunctive 1
Asir, to seize	asido: asiendo	yo asiera
		tú asieras
Present	**Future**	él asiera
yo asgo	yo asiré	nos'os asiéramos
tú ases	tú asirás	vos'os asierais
él ase	él asirá	ellos asieran
nos'os asimos	nos'os asiremos	
vos'os asís	vos'os asiréis	**Imp'fect-sub've 2**
ellos asen	ellos asirán	yo asiese
		tú asieses
Imperfect	**Conditional**	él asiese
yo asía	yo asiría	nos'os asiésemos
tú asías	tú asirías	vos'os asieseis
él asía	él asiría	ellos asiesen
nos'os asíamos	nos'os asiríamos	
vos'os asíais	vos'os asiríais	**Imperative-Do**
ellos asían	ellos asirían	(tú) ase
		(él) asga
Preterite	**Present subj've**	(nos'os) asgamos
yo así	yo asga	(vos'os) asid
tú asiste	tú asgas	(ellos) asgan
él asió	él asga	
nos'os asimos	nos'os asgamos	**Imperative-Don't**
vos'os asisteis	vos'os asgáis	no asgas
ellos asieron	ellos asgan	no asga
		no asgamos
Comp'nd tenses- 63-I-Haber +Past-P		no asgáis
		no asgan

78

57-I-Caber

Note: present. preterite. future. conditional. present subjunctive. imperfect-subjunctive. imperative.

Verb infinitive	Participles	Imperfect-subjunctive 1
Caber, to fit, to accommodate	cabido: cabiendo	yo cupiera
		tú cupieras
Present	**Future**	él cupiera
yo quepo	yo cabré	nos'os cupiéramos
tú cabes	tú cabrás	vos'os cupierais
él cabe	él cabrá	ellos cupieran
nos'os cabemos	nos'os cabremos	
vos'os cabéis	vos'os cabréis	**Imp'fect-sub've 2**
ellos caben	ellos cabrán	yo cupiese
		tú cupieses
Imperfect	**Conditional**	él cupiese
yo cabía	yo cabría	nos'os cupiésemos
tú cabías	tú cabrías	vos'os cupieseis
él cabía	él cabría	ellos cupiesen
nos'os cabíamos	nos'os cabríamos	
vos'os cabíais	vos'os cabríais	**Imperative-Do**
ellos cabían	ellos cabrían	(tú) cabe
		(él) quepa
Preterite	**Present subj've**	(nos'os) quepamos
yo cupe	yo quepa	(vos'os) cabed
tú cupiste	tú quepas	(ellos) quepan
él cupo	él quepa	
nos'os cupimos	nos'os quepamos	**Imperative-Don't**
vos'os cupisteis	vos'os quepáis	no quepas
ellos cupieron	ellos quepan	no quepa
		no quepamos
Comp'nd tenses- 63-I-Haber +Past-P		no quepáis
		no quepan

79

58-I-Cocer

Note: present. present subjunctive. imperative.

Verb infinitive	Participles	Imperfect-subjunctive 1
Cocer, to cook	cocido: cociendo	yo cociera
		tú cocieras
Present	**Future**	él cociera
yo cuezo	yo coceré	nos'os cociéramos
tú cueces	tú cocerás	vos'os cocierais
él cuece	él cocerá	ellos cocieran
nos'os cocemos	nos'os coceremos	
vos'os cocéis	vos'os coceréis	**Imp'fect-sub've 2**
ellos cuecen	ellos cocerán	yo cociese
		tú cocieses
Imperfect	**Conditional**	él cociese
yo cocía	yo cocería	nos'os cociésemos
tú cocías	tú cocerías	vos'os cocieseis
él cocía	él cocería	ellos cociesen
nos'os cocíamos	nos'os coceríamos	
vos'os cocíais	vos'os coceríais	**Imperative-Do**
ellos cocían	ellos cocerían	(tú) cuece
		(él) cueza
Preterite	**Present subj've**	(nos'os) cozamos
yo cocí	**Present**	(vos'os) coced
tú cociste	yo cueza	(ellos) cuezan
él coció	tú cuezas	
nos'os cocimos	él cueza	**Imperative-Don't**
vos'os cocisteis	nos'os cozamos	no cuezas
ellos cocieron	vos'os cozáis	no cueza
	ellos cuezan	no cozamos
Comp'nd tenses- 63-I-Haber +Past-P		no cozáis
		no cuezan

59-I-Dar

Note: present. preterite. present subjunctive. imperfect-subjunctive. imperative.

Verb infinitive	Participles	Imperfect-subjunctive 1
Dar, to give	dado: dando	yo diera
		tú dieras
Present	**Future**	él diera
yo doy	yo daré	nos'os diéramos
tú das	tú darás	vos'os dierais
él da	él dará	ellos dieran
nos'os damos	nos'os daremos	
vos'os dais	vos'os daréis	**Imp'fect-sub've 2**
ellos dan	ellos darán	yo diese
		tú dieses
Imperfect	**Conditional**	él diese
yo daba	yo daría	nos'os diésemos
tú dabas	tú darías	vos'os dieseis
él daba	él daría	ellos diesen
nos'os dábamos	nos'os daríamos	
vos'os dabais	vos'os daríais	**Imperative-Do**
ellos daban	ellos darían	(tú) da
		(él) dé
Preterite	**Present subj've**	(nos'os) demos
yo di	yo dé	(vos'os) dad
tú diste	tú des	(ellos) den
él dio	él dé	
nos'os dimos	nos'os demos	**Imperative-Don't**
vos'os disteis	vos'os deis	no des
ellos dieron	ellos den	no dé
		no demos
Comp'nd tenses- 63-I-Haber +Past-P		no deis
		no den

81

60-I-Decir

Note: present. preterite. future. conditional. present subjunctive. imperfect-subjunctive. imperative.

Verb infinitive	Participles	Imperfect-subjunctive 1
Decir, to say	dicho: diciendo	yo dijera
		tú dijeras
Present	**Future**	él dijera
yo digo	yo diré	nos'os dijéramos
tú dices	tú dirás	vos'os dijerais
él dice	él dirá	ellos dijeran
nos'os decimos	nos'os diremos	
vos'os decís	vos'os diréis	**Imp'fect-sub've 2**
ellos dicen	ellos dirán	yo dijese
		tú dijeses
Imperfect	**Conditional**	él dijese
yo decía	yo diría	nos'os dijésemos
tú decías	tú dirías	vos'os dijeseis
él decía	él diría	ellos dijesen
nos'os decíamos	nos'os diríamos	
vos'os decíais	vos'os diríais	**Imperative-Do**
ellos decían	ellos dirían	(tú) di
		(él) diga
Preterite	**Present subj've**	(nos'os) digamos
yo dije	yo diga	(vos'os) decid
tú dijiste	tú digas	(ellos) digan
él dijo	él diga	
nos'os dijimos	nos'os digamos	**Imperative-Don't**
vos'os dijisteis	vos'os digáis	no digas
ellos dijeron	ellos digan	no diga
		no digamos
Comp'nd tenses- 63-I-Haber +Past-P		no digáis
		no digan

61-I-Errar

Verb infinitive	Participles	Imperfect-subjunctive 1
Errar, to miss, to fail, to get wrong	errado: errando	yo errara
		tú erraras
Present	**Future**	él errara
yo yerro	yo erraré	nos'os erráramos
tú yerras	tú errarás	vos'os errarais
él yerra	él errará	ellos erraran
nos'os erramos	nos'os erraremos	
vos'os erráis	vos'os erraréis	**Imp'fect-sub've 2**
ellos yerran	ellos errarán	yo errase
		tú errases
Imperfect	**Conditional**	él errase
yo erraba	yo erraría	nos'os errásemos
tú errabas	tú errarías	vos'os erraseis
él erraba	él erraría	ellos errasen
nos'os errábamos	nos'os erraríamos	
vos'os errabais	vos'os erraríais	**Imperative-Do**
ellos erraban	ellos errarían	(tú) yerra
		(él) yerre
Preterite	**Present subj've**	(nos'os) erremos
yo erré	yo yerre	(vos'os) errad
tú erraste	tú yerres	(ellos) yerren
él erró	él yerre	
nos'os erramos	nos'os erremos	**Imperative-Don't**
vos'os errasteis	vos'os erréis	no yerres
ellos erraron	ellos yerren	no yerre
		no erremos
Comp'nd tenses-63-I-Haber +Past-P		no erréis
		no yerren

83

62-I-Estar

Note: present. preterite. present subjunctive. imperfect-subjunctive. imperative.

Verb infinitive	Participles	Imperfect-subjunctive 1
Estar, to be	estado: estando	yo estuviera
		tú estuvieras
Present	**Future**	él estuviera
yo estoy	yo estaré	nos'os estuviéramos
tú estás	tú estarás	vos'os estuvierais
él está	él estará	ellos estuvieran
nos'os estamos	nos'os estaremos	
vos'os estáis	vos'os estaréis	**Imp'fect-sub've 2**
ellos están	ellos estarán	**Imperfect-subjunctive**
		yo estuviese
Imperfect	**Conditional**	tú estuvieses
yo estaba	yo estaría	él estuviese
tú estabas	tú estarías	nos'os estuviésemos
él estaba	él estaría	vos'os estuvieseis
nos'os estábamos	nos'os estaríamos	ellos estuviesen
vos'os estabais	vos'os estaríais	**Imperative-Do**
ellos estaban	ellos estarían	(tú) está
		(él) esté
Preterite	**Present subj've**	(nos'os) estemos
yo estuve	yo esté	(vos'os) estad
tú estuviste	tú estés	(ellos) estén
él estuvo	él esté	
nos'os estuvimos	nos'os estemos	**Imperative-Don't**
vos'os estuvisteis	vos'os estéis	no estés
ellos estuvieron	ellos estén	no esté
		no estemos
Comp'nd tenses-63-I-Haber +Past-P		no estéis
		no estén

84

63(a)-I-Haber (auxillary verb) Note present. preterite. future. conditional. present subjunctive. imperfect-subjunctive. imperative.

Verb infinitive	Participles	
Haber, to have	habido: habiendo	
Present-Perfect	**Present-Perfect subjunctive**	**Future Perfect**
yo he+Past-P	yo haya+Past-P	yo habré+Past-P
tú has+Past-P	tú hayas+Past-P	tú habrás+Past-P
él ha+Past-P; hay	él haya+Past-P	él habrá+Past-P
nos'os hemos+Past-P	nos'os hayamos+ Past-P	nos'os habremos+Past-P
vos'os habéis+Past-P	vos'os hayáis+Past-P	vos'os habréis+ Past-P
ellos han+Past-P	ellos hayan+Past-P	ellos habrán+Past-P
Pluperfect	**Pluperfect subjunctive 1**	**Conditional Perfect**
yo había+Past-P	yo hubiera+Past-P	yo habría+Past-P
tú habías+Past-P	tú hubieras+Past-P	tú habrías+Past-P
él había+Past-P	él hubiera+Past-P	él habría+Past-P
nos'os habíamos+Past-P	nos'os hubiéramos+Past-P	nos'os habríamos+Past-P
vos'os habíais+Past-P	vos'os hubierais+Past-P	vos'os habríais+ Past-P
ellos habían+Past-P	ellos hubieran+ Past-P	ellos habrían+Past-P
Preterite Perfect	**Pluperfect-subjunctive 2**	
yo hube+Past-P	yo hubiese+Past-P	
tú hubiste+Past-P	tú hubieses+Past-P	
él hubo+Past-P	él hubiese+Past-P	
nos'os hubimos+ Past-P	nos'os hubiésemos+Past-P	
vos'os hubisteis+ Past-P	vos'os hubieseis+Past-P	
ellos hubieron+ Past-P	ellos hubiesen+ Past-P	

63(b)-I-RF-Haber(auxillary verb) used with reflexive verb
Note present. preterite. future. conditional. present subjunctive. imperfect-subjunctive. imperative

Verb infinitive	Participles	
Haber, to have: (reflexive form)	habido: habiendo	
Present-Perfect	**Present-Perfect subjunctive**	**Future Perfect**
me he+Past-P	me haya+Past-P	me habré+Past-P
te has+Past-P	te hayas+Past-P	te habrás+Past-P
se ha+Past-P	se haya+Past-P	se habrá+Past-P
nos hemos+Past-P	nos hayamos+Past-P	nos habremos+Past-P
vos habéis+Past-P	vos hayáis+Past-P	vos habréis+Past-P
se han+Past-P	se hayan+Past-P	se habrán+Past-P
Pluperfect	**Pluperfect subjunctive 1**	**Conditional Perfect**
me había+Past-P	yo hubiera+Past-P	me habría+Past-P
te habías+Past-P	tú hubieras+Past-P	te habrías+Past-P
se había+Past-P	él hubiera+Past-P	se habría+Past-P
nos habíamos+Past-P	nos'os hubiéramos+Past-P	nos habríamos+Past-P
vos habíais+Past-P	vos'os hubierais+Past-P	vos habríais+Past-P
se habían+Past-P	ellos hubieran+Past-P	se habrían+Past-P
Preterite Perfect	**Pluperfect-subjunctive 2**	
me hube+Past-P	yo hubiese+Past-P	
te hubiste+Past-P	tú hubieses+Past-P	
se hubo+Past-P	él hubiese+Past-P	
nos hubimos+Past-P	nos'os hubiésemos+Past-P	
vos hubisteis+Past-P	vos'os hubieseis+Past-P	
se hubieron+Past-P	ellos hubiesen+Past-P	

64-I-Hacer

Note: participles. present. preterite. future. conditional. present subjunctive. imperfect-subjunctive. imperative.

Verb infinitive	Participles	Imperfect-subjunctive 1
Hacer, to make, to do	hecho: haciendo	yo hiciera
		tú hicieras
Present	**Future**	él hiciera
yo hago	yo haré	nos'os hiciéramos
tú haces	tú harás	vos'os hicierais
él hace	él hará	ellos hicieran
nos'os hacemos	nos'os haremos	
vos'os hacéis	vos'os haréis	**Imp'fect-sub've 2**
ellos hacen	ellos harán	yo hiciese
		tú hicieses
Imperfect	**Conditional**	él hiciese
yo hacía	yo haría	nos'os hiciésemos
tú hacías	tú harías	vos'os hicieseis
él hacía	él haría	ellos hiciesen
nos'os hacíamos	nos'os haríamos	
vos'os hacíais	vos'os haríais	**Imperative-Do**
ellos hacían	ellos harían	(tú) haz
		(él) haga
Preterite	**Present subj've**	(nos'os) hagamos
yo hice	yo haga	(vos'os) haced
tú hiciste	tú hagas	(ellos) hagan
él hizo	él haga	
nos'os hicimos	nos'os hagamos	**Imperative-Don't**
vos'os hicisteis	vos'os hagáis	no hagas
ellos hicieron	ellos hagan	no haga
		no hagamos
Comp'nd tenses- 63-I-Haber +Past-P		no hagáis
		no hagan

87

65-I-Ir

Note: participles. present. preterite. imperfect. present subjunctive. imperfect-subjunctive. imperative.

Verb infinitive	Participles	Imperfect-subjunctive 1
Ir, to go	ido: yendo	yo fuera
		tú fueras
Present	**Future**	él fuera
yo voy	yo iré	nos'os fuéramos
tú vas	tú irás	vos'os fuerais
él va	él irá	ellos fueran
nos'os vamos	nos'os iremos	
vos'os vais	vos'os iréis	**Imp'fect-sub've 2**
ellos van	ellos irán	yo fuese
		tú fueses
Imperfect	**Conditional**	él fuese
yo iba	yo iría	nos'os fuésemos
tú ibas	tú irías	vos'os fueseis
él iba	él iría	ellos fuesen
nos'os íbamos	nos'os iríamos	
vos'os ibais	vos'os iríais	**Imperative-Do**
ellos iban	ellos irían	(tú) ve
		(él) vaya
Preterite	**Present subj've**	(nos'os) vamos;
yo fui	yo vaya	(vos'os) id
tú fuiste	tú vayas	(ellos) vayan
él fue	él vaya	
nos'os fuimos	nos'os vayamos	**Imperative-Don't**
vos'os fuisteis	vos'os vayáis	no vayas
ellos fueron	ellos vayan	no vaya
		no vayamos
Comp'nd tenses- 63-I-Haber +Past-P		no vayáis
		no vayan

88

66-I-Oir

Note: participles. present. preterite. present subjunctive. imperfect-subjunctive. imperative.

Verb infinitive	Participles	Imperfect-subjunctive 1
Oir, to hear	oído: oyendo	yo oyera
		tú oyeras
Present	**Future**	él oyera
yo oigo	yo oiré	nos'os oyéramos
tú oyes	tú oirás	vos'os oyerais
él oye	él oirá	ellos oyeran
nos'os oímos	nos'os oiremos	
vos'os oís	vos'os oiréis	**Imp'fect-sub've 2**
ellos oyen	ellos oirán	yo oyese
		tú oyeses
Imperfect	**Conditional**	él oyese
yo oía	yo oiría	nos'os oyésemos
tú oías	tú oirías	vos'os oyeseis
él oía	él oiría	ellos oyesen
nos'os oíamos	nos'os oiríamos	
vos'os oíais	vos'os oiríais	**Imperative-Do**
ellos oían	ellos oirían	(tú) oye
		(él) oiga
Preterite	**Present subj've**	(nos'os) oigamos
yo oí	yo oiga	(vos'os) oíd
tú oíste	tú oigas	(ellos) oigan
él oyó	él oiga	
nos'os oímos	nos'os oigamos	**Imperative-Don't**
vos'os oísteis	vos'os oigáis	no oigas
ellos oyeron	ellos oigan	no oiga
		no oigamos
Comp'nd tenses- 63-I-Haber +Past-P		no oigáis
		no oigan

67-I-Poder

Note: present. preterite. future. conditional. present subjunctive. imperfect-subjunctive. imperative.

Verb infinitive	Participles	Imperfect-subjunctive 1
Poder, to be able to	podido: podiendo	yo pudiera
		tú pudieras
Present	**Future**	él pudiera
yo puedo	yo podré	nos'os pudiéramos
tú puedes	tú podrás	vos'os pudierais
él puede	él podrá	ellos pudieran
nos'os podemos	nos'os podremos	
vos'os podéis	vos'os podréis	**Imp'fect-sub've 2**
ellos pueden	ellos podrán	yo pudiese
		tú pudieses
Imperfect	**Conditional**	él pudiese
yo podía	yo podría	nos'os pudiésemos
tú podías	tú podrías	vos'os pudieseis
él podía	él podría	ellos pudiesen
nos'os podíamos	nos'os podríamos	
vos'os podíais	vos'os podríais	**Imperative-Do**
ellos podían	ellos podrían	(tú) puede
		(él) pueda
Preterite	**Present subj've**	(nos'os) podamos
yo pude	yo pueda	(vos'os) poded
tú pudiste	tú puedas	(ellos) puedan
él pudo	él pueda	
nos'os pudimos	nos'os podamos	**Imperative-Don't**
vos'os pudisteis	vos'os podáis	no puedas
ellos pudieron	ellos puedan	no pueda
		no podamos
Comp'nd tenses- 63-I-Haber +Past-P		no podáis
		no puedan

90

68-I-Poner

Note: participles. present. preterite. future. conditional. present subjunctive imperfect-subjunctive. imperative.

Verb infinitive	Participles	Imperfect-subjunctive 1
Poner, to put, to place	puesto: poniendo	yo pusiera
		tú pusieras
Present	**Future**	él pusiera
yo pongo	yo pondré	nos'os pusiéramos
tú pones	tú pondrás	vos'os pusierais
él pone	él pondrá	ellos pusieran
nos'os ponemos	nos'os pondremos	
vos'os ponéis	vos'os pondréis	**Imp'fect-sub've 2**
ellos ponen	ellos pondrán	yo pusiese
		tú pusieses
Imperfect	**Conditional**	él pusiese
yo ponía	yo pondría	nos'os pusiésemos
tú ponías	tú pondrías	vos'os pusieseis
él ponía	él pondría	ellos pusiesen
nos'os poníamos	nos'os pondríamos	
vos'os poníais	vos'os pondríais	**Imperative-Do**
ellos ponían	ellos pondrían	(tú) pon
		(él) ponga
Preterite	**Present subj've**	(nos'os) pongamos
yo puse	yo ponga	(vos'os) poned
tú pusiste	tú pongas	(ellos) pongan
él puso	él ponga	
nos'os pusimos	nos'os pongamos	**Imperative-Don't**
vos'os pusisteis	vos'os pongáis	no pongas
ellos pusieron	ellos pongan	no ponga
		no pongamos
Comp'nd tenses- 63-I-Haber +Past-P		no pongáis
		no pongan

69-I-Querer

Note: present. preterite. future. conditional. present subjunctive. imperfect-subjunctive. imperative.

Verb infinitive	Participles	Imperfect-subjunctive 1
Querer, to want, to love	querido: queriendo	yo quisiera
		tú quisieras
Present	**Future**	él quisiera
yo quiero	yo querré	nos'os quisiéramos
tú quieres	tú querrás	vos'os quisierais
él quiere	él querrá	ellos quisieran
nos'os queremos	nos'os querremos	
vos'os queréis	vos'os querréis	**Imp'fect-sub've 2**
ellos quieren	ellos querrán	yo quisiere
		tú quisieres
Imperfect	**Conditional**	él quisiere
yo quería	yo querría	nos'os quisiéremos
tú querías	tú querrías	vos'os quisiereis
él quería	él querría	ellos quisieren
nos'os queríamos	nos'os querríamos	
vos'os queríais	vos'os querríais	**Imperative-Do**
ellos querían	ellos querrían	(tú) quiere
		(él) quiera
Preterite	**Present subj've**	(nos'os) queramos
yo quise	yo quiera	(vos'os) quered
tú quisiste	tú quieras	(ellos) quieran
él quiso	él quiera	
nos'os quisimos	nos'os queramos	**Imperative-Don't**
vos'os quisisteis	vos'os queráis	no quieras
ellos quisieron	ellos quieran	no quiera
		no queramos
Comp'nd tenses- 63-I-Haber +Past-P		no queráis
		no quieran

70-I-Roer

Verb infinitive	Participles	Imperfect-subjunctive 1
Roer, to gnaw, to nibble	roído: royendo	yo royera
		tú royeras
Present	**Future**	él royera
yo roigo	yo roeré	nos'os royéramos
tú roes	tú roerás	vos'os royerais
él roe	él roerá	ellos royeran
nos'os roemos	nos'os roeremos	
vos'os roéis	vos'os roeréis	**Imp'fect-sub've 2**
ellos roen	ellos roerán	yo royese
		tú royeses
Imperfect	**Conditional**	él royese
yo roía	yo roería	nos'os royésemos
tú roías	tú roerías	vos'os royeseis
él roía	é roería	ellos royesen
nos'os roíamos	nos'os roeríamos	
vos'os roíais	vos'os roeríais	**Imperative-Do**
ellos roían	ellos roerían	(tú) roe
		(él) roiga
Preterite	**Present subj've**	(nos'os) roigamos
yo roí	yo roiga	(vos'os) roed
tú roíste	tú roigas	(ellos) roigan
él royó	él roiga	
nos'os roímos	nos'os roigamos	**Imperative-Don't**
vos'os roísteis	vos'os roigáis	no roigas
ellos royeron	ellos roigan	no roiga
		no roigamos
Comp'nd tenses- 63-I-Haber +Past-P		no roigáis
		no roigan

71-I-Saber

Note: present. preterite. future. conditional. present subjunctive. imperfect-subjunctive. imperative.

Verb infinitive	Participles	Imperfect-subjunctive 1
Saber, to know	sabido: sabiendo	yo supiera
		tú supieras
Present	**Future**	él supiera
yo sé	yo sabré	nos'os supiéramos
tú sabes	tú sabrás	vos'os supierais
él sabe	él sabrá	ellos supieran
nos'os sabemos	nos'os sabremos	
vos'os sabéis	vos'os sabréis	**Imp'fect-sub've 2**
ellos saben	ellos sabrán	yo supiese
		tú supieses
Imperfect	**Conditional**	él supiese
yo sabía	yo sabría	nos'os supiésemos
tú sabías	tú sabrías	vos'os supieseis
él sabía	él sabría	ellos supiesen
nos'os sabíamos	nos'os sabríamos	
vos'os sabíais	vos'os sabríais	**Imperative-Do**
ellos sabían	ellos sabrían	(tú) sabe
		(él) sepa
Preterite	**Present subj've**	(nos'os) sepamos
yo supe	yo sepa	(vos'os) sabed
tú supiste	tú sepas	(ellos) sepan
él supo	él sepa	
nos'os supimos	nos'os sepamos	**Imperative-Don't**
vos'os supisteis	vos'os sepáis	no sepas
ellos supieron	ellos sepan	no sepa
		no sepamos
Comp'nd tenses-63-I-Haber +Past-P		no sepáis
		no sepan

72-I-Salir
Note: present. future. conditional. present subjunctive. imperative.

Verb infinitive	Participles	Imperfect-subjunctive 1
Salir, to leave, to go out	salido: saliendo	yo saliera
		tú salieras
Present	**Future**	él saliera
yo salgo	yo saldré	nos'os saliéramos
tú sales	tú saldrás	vos'os salierais
él sale	él saldrá	ellos salieran
nos'os salimos	nos'os saldremos	
vos'os salís	vos'os saldréis	**Imp'fect-sub've 2**
ellos salen	ellos saldrán	yo saliese
		tú salieses
Imperfect	**Conditional**	él saliese
yo salía	yo saldría	nos'os saliésemos
tú salías	tú saldrías	vos'os salieseis
él salía	él saldría	ellos saliesen
nos'os salíamos	nos'os saldríamos	
vos'os salíais	vos'os saldríais	**Imperative-Do**
ellos salían	ellos saldrían	(tú) sal
		(él) salga
Preterite	**Present subj've**	(nos'os) salgamos
yo salí	yo salga	(vos'os) salid
tú saliste	tú salgas	(ellos) salgan
él salió	él salga	
nos'os salimos	nos'os salgamos	**Imperative-Don't**
vos'os salisteis	vos'os salgáis	no salgas
ellos salieron	ellos salgan	no salga
		no salgamos
Comp'nd tenses-63-I-Haber +Past-P		no salgáis
		no salgan

73-I-Satisfacer

Note: participles. present. preterite. future. conditional. present subjunctive. imperfect-subjunctive. imperative.

Verb infinitive	Participles	Imperfect-subjunctive 1
Satisfacer, to satisfy	satisfecho: satisfaciendo	yo satisficiera
		tú satisficieras
Present	**Future**	él satisficiera
yo satisfago	yo satisfaré	nos'os satisficiéramos
tú satisfaces	tú satisfarás	vos'os satisficierais
él satisface	él satisfará	ellos satisficieran
nos'os satisfacemos	nos'os satisfaremos	
vos'os satisfacéis	vos'os satisfaréis	**Imp'fect-sub've 2**
ellos satisfacen	ellos satisfarán	yo satisficiese
		tú satisficieses
Imperfect	**Conditional**	él satisficiese
yo satisfacía	yo satisfaría	nos'os satisficiésemos
tú satisfacías	tú satisfarías	vos'os satisficieseis
él satisfacía	él satisfaría	ellos satisficiesen
nos'os satisfacíamos	nos'os satisfaríamos	
vos'os satisfacíais	vos'os satisfaríais	**Imperative-Do**
ellos satisfacían	ellos satisfarían	(tú) satisface;
		(él) satisfaga
Preterite	**Present subj've**	(nos'os) satisfagamos
yo satisfice	yo satisfaga	(vos'os) satisfaced
tú satisficiste	tú satisfagas	(ellos) satisfagan
él satisfizo	él satisfaga	
nos'os satisficimos	nos'os satisfagamos	**Imperative-Don't**
vos'os satisficisteis	vos'os satisfagáis	no satisfagas
ellos satisficieron	ellos satisfagan	no satisfaga
		no satisfagamos
Comp'nd tenses- 63-I-Haber +Past-P		no satisfagáis
		no satisfagan

74-I-Ser

Note: present. preterite. imperfect. present subjunctive. imperfect-subjunctive. imperative.

Verb infinitive	Participles	Imperfect-subjunctive 1
Ser, to be	sido: siendo	yo fuera
		tú fueras
Present	**Future**	él fuera
yo soy	yo seré	nos'os fuéramos
tú eres	tú serás	vos'os fuerais
él es	él será	ellos fueran
nos'os somos	nos'os seremos	
vos'os sois	vos'os seréis	**Imp'fect-sub've 2**
ellos son	ellos serán	yo fuese
		tú fueses
Imperfect	**Conditional**	él fuese
yo era	yo sería	nos'os fuésemos
tú eras	tú serías	vos'os fueseis
él era	él sería	ellos fuesen
nos'os éramos	nos'os seríamos	
vos'os erais	vos'os seríais	**Imperative-Do**
ellos eran	ellos serían	(tú) sé
		(él) sea
Preterite	**Present subj've**	(nos'os) seamos
yo fui	yo sea	(vos'os) sed
tú fuiste	tú seas	(ellos) sean
él fue	él sea	
nos'os fuimos	nos'os seamos	**Imperative-Don't**
vos'os fuisteis	vos'os seáis	no seas
ellos fueron	ellos sean	no sea
		no seamos
Comp'nd tenses- 63-I-Haber +Past-P		no seáis
		no sean

75-I-Tener

Note: present. preterite. future. conditional. present subjunctive. imperfect-subjunctive. imperative.

Verb infinitive	Participles	Imperfect-subjunctive 1
Tener, to have	tenido: teniendo	yo tuviera
		tú tuvieras
Present	**Future**	él tuviera
yo tengo	yo tendré	nos'os tuviéramos
tú tienes	tú tendrás	vos'os tuvierais
él tiene	él tendrá	ellos tuvieran
nos'os tenemos	nos'os tendremos	
vos'os tenéis	vos'os tendréis	**Imp'fect-sub've 2**
ellos tienen	ellos tendrán	yo tuviese
		tú tuvieses
Imperfect	**Conditional**	él tuviese
yo tenía	yo tendría	nos'os tuviésemos
tú tenías	tú tendrías	vos'os tuvieseis
él tenía	él tendría	ellos tuviesen
nos'os teníamos	nos'os tendríamos	
vos'os teníais	vos'os tendríais	**Imperative-Do**
ellos tenían	ellos tendrían	(tú) ten
		(él) tenga
Preterite	**Present subj've**	(nos'os) tengamos
yo tuve	yo tenga	(vos'os) tened
tú tuviste	tú tengas	(ellos) tengan
él tuvo	él tenga	
nos'os tuvimos	nos'os tengamos	**Imperative-Don't**
vos'os tuvisteis	vos'os tengáis	no tengas
ellos tuvieron	ellos tengan	no tenga
		no tengamos
Comp'nd tenses- 63-I-Haber +Past-P		no tengáis
		no tengan

76-I-Traer

Note: participles. present. preterite. imperfect. future. conditional. present subjunctive. imperfect-subjunctive. imperative.

Verb infinitive	Participles	Imperfect-subjunctive 1
Traer, to bring	traído: trayendo	yo trajera
		tú trajeras
Present	**Future**	él trajera
yo traigo	yo traeré	nos'os trajéramos
tú traes	tú traerás	vos'os trajerais
él trae	él traerá	ellos trajeran
nos'os traemos	nos'os traeremos	
vos'os traéis	vos'os traeréis	**Imp'fect-sub've 2**
ellos traen	ellos traerán	yo trajese
		tú trajeses
Imperfect	**Conditional**	él trajese
yo traía	yo traería	nos'os trajésemos
tú traías	tú traerías	vos'os trajeseis
él traía	él traería	ellos trajesen
nos'os traíamos	nos'os traeríamos	
vos'os traíais	vos'os traeríais	**Imperative-Do**
ellos traían	ellos traerían	(tú) trae
		(él) traiga
Preterite	**Present subj've**	(nos'os) traigamos
yo traje	yo traiga	(vos'os) traed
tú trajiste	tú traigas	(ellos) traigan
él trajo	él traiga	
nos'os trajimos	nos'os traigamos	**Imperative-Don't**
vos'os trajisteis	vos'os traigáis	no traigas
ellos trajeron	ellos traigan	no traiga
		no traigamos
Comp'nd tenses- 63-I-Haber +Past-P		no traigáis
		no traigan

99

77-I-Valer

Note: present. future. conditional. present subjunctive. imperative.

Verb infinitive	Participles	Imperfect-subjunctive 1
Valer, to cost, to be worth	valido: valiendo	yo valiera
		tú valieras
Present	**Future**	él valiera
yo valgo	yo valdré	nos'os valiéramos
tú vales	tú valdrás	vos'os valierais
él vale	él valdrá	ellos valieran
nos'os valemos	nos'os valdremos	
vos'os valéis	vos'os valdréis	**Imp'fect-sub've 2**
ellos valen	ellos valdrán	yo valiese
		tú valieses
Imperfect	**Conditional**	él valiese
yo valía	yo valdría	nos'os valiésemos
tú valías	tú valdrías	vos'os valieseis
él valía	él valdría	ellos valiesen
nos'os valíamos	nos'os valdríamos	
vos'os valíais	vos'os valdríais	**Imperative-Do**
ellos valían	ellos valdrían	(tú) vale; val
		(él) valga
Preterite	**Present subj've**	(nos'os) valgamos
yo valí	yo valga	(vos'os) valed
tú valiste	tú valgas	(ellos) valgan
él valió	él valga	
nos'os valimos	nos'os valgamos	**Imperative-Don't**
vos'os valisteis	vos'os valgáis	no valgas
ellos valieron	ellos valgan	no valga
		no valgamos
Comp'nd tenses- 63-I-Haber +Past-P		no valgáis
		no valgan

78-I-Venir

Note: participles. present. preterite. future. conditional. present subjunctive. imperfect-subjunctive. imperative.

Verb infinitive	Participles	Imperfect-subjunctive 1
Venir, to come	venido: viniendo	yo viniera
		tú vinieras
Present	**Future**	él viniera
yo vengo	yo vendré	nos'os viniéramos
tú vienes	tú vendrás	vos'os vinierais
él viene	él vendrá	ellos vinieran
nos'os venimos	nos'os vendremos	
vos'os venís	vos'os vendréis	**Imp'fect-sub've 2**
ellos vienen	ellos vendrán	yo viniese
		tú vinieses
Imperfect	**Conditional**	él viniese
yo venía	yo vendría	nos'os viniésemos
tú venías	tú vendrías	vos'os vinieseis
él venía	él vendría	ellos viniesen
nos'os veníamos	nos'os vendríamos	
vos'os veníais	vos'os vendríais	**Imperative-Do**
ellos venían	ellos vendrían	(tú) ven
		(él) venga
Preterite	**Present subj've**	(nos'os) vengamos
yo vine	yo venga	(vos'os) venid
tú viniste	tú vengas	(ellos) vengan
él vino	él venga	
nos'os vinimos	nos'os vengamos	**Imperative-Don't**
vos'os vinisteis	vos'os vengáis	no vengas
ellos vinieron	ellos vengan	no venga
		no vengamos
Comp'nd tenses- 63-I-Haber +Past-P		no vengáis
		no vengan

79-I-Ver

Note: participles. present. preterite. present subjunctive. imperative.

Verb infinitive	Participles	Imperfect-subjunctive 1
Ver, to see	visto: viendo	yo viera
		tú vieras
Present	**Future**	él viera
yo veo	yo veré	nos'os viéramos
tú ves	tú verás	vos'os vierais
él ve	él verá	ellos vieran
nos'os vemos	nos'os veremos	
vos'os veis	vos'os veréis	**Imp'fect-sub've 2**
ellos ven	ellos verán	yo viese
		tú vieses
Imperfect	**Conditional**	él viese
yo veía	yo vería	nos'os viésemos
tú veías	tú verías	vos'os vieseis
él veía	él vería	ellos viesen
nos'os veíamos	nos'os veríamos	
vos'os veíais	vos'os veríais	**Imperative-Do**
ellos veían	ellos verían	(tú) ve
		(él) vea
Preterite	**Present subj've**	(nos'os) veamos
yo vi	yo vea	(vos'os) ved
tú viste	tú veas	(ellos) vean
él vio	él vea	
nos'os vimos	nos'os veamos	**Imperative-Don't**
vos'os visteis	vos'os veáis	no veas
ellos vieron	ellos vean	no vea
		no veamos
Comp'nd tenses- 63-I-Haber +Past-P		no veáis
		no vean

80-M-Agorar
Note: present. present subjunctive. imperative.
The o would become ue where it is accented, (as in **26-S-Aprobar-Acortar**) but with agorar the resulting gu becomes gü in front of e to preserve the correct sound.

Verb infinitive	Participles	Imperfect-subjunctive 1
Agorar, to bode, to be an omen of.	agorado: agorando	yo agorara
		tú agoraras
Present	**Future**	él agorara
yo agüero	yo agoraré	nos'os agoráramos
tú agüeras	tú agorarás	vos'os agorarais
él agüera	él agorará	ellos agoraran
nos'os agoramos	nos'os agoraremos	
vos'os agoráis	vos'os agoraréis	**Imp'fect-sub've 2**
ellos agüeran	ellos agorarán	yo agorase
		tú agorases
Imperfect	**Conditional**	él agorase
yo agoraba	yo agoraría	nos'os agorásemos
tú agorabas	tú agorarías	vos'os agoraseis
él agoraba	él agoraría	ellos agorasen
nos'os agorábamos	nos'os agoraríamos	
vos'os agorabais	vos'os agoraríais	**Imperative-Do**
ellos agoraban	ellos agorarían	(tú) agüera
		(él) agüere
Preterite	**Present subj've**	(nos'os) agoremos
yo agoré	yo agüere	(vos'os) agorad
tú agoraste	tú agüeres	(ellos) agüeren
él agoró	él agüere	
nos'os agoramos	nos'os agoremos	**Imperative-Don't**
vos'os agorasteis	vos'os agoréis	no agüeres
ellos agoraron	ellos agüeren	no agüere
		no agoremos
Comp'nd tenses- 63-I-Haber +Past-P		no agoréis
		no agüeren

103

81-M-Almorzar

Note: present. preterite. present subjunctive. imperative.

Also see/compare verb types: **7-O-Rezar** and **26-S-Aprobar-Acortar**

Verb infinitive	Participles	Imperfect-subjunctive 1
Almorzar, to have lunch	almorzado: almorzando	yo almorzara
		tú almorzaras
Present	**Future**	él almorzara
yo almuerzo	yo almorzaré	nos'os almorzáramos
tú almuerzas	tú almorzarás	vos'os almorzarais
él almuerza	él almorzará	ellos almorzaran
nos'os almorzamos	nos'os almorzaremos	
vos'os almorzáis	vos'os almorzaréis	**Imp'fect-sub've 2**
ellos almuerzan	ellos almorzarán	yo almorzase
		tú almorzases
Imperfect	**Conditional**	él almorzase
yo almorzaba	yo almorzaría	nos'os almorzásemos
tú almorzabas	tú almorzarías	vos'os almorzaseis
él almorzaba	él almorzaría	ellos almorzasen
nos'os almorzábamos	nos'os almorzaríamos	
vos'os almorzabais	vos'os almorzaríais	**Imperative-Do**
ellos almorzaban	ellos almorzarían	(tú) almuerza
		(él) almuerce
Preterite	**Present subj've**	(nos'os) almorcemos
yo almorcé	yo almuerce	(vos'os) almorzad
tú almorzaste	tú almuerces	(ellos) almuercen
él almorzó	él almuerce	
nos'os almorzamos	nos'os almorcemos	**Imperative-Don't**
vos'os almorzasteis	vos'os almorcéis	no almuerces
ellos almorzaron	ellos almuercen	no almuerce
		no almorcemos
Comp'nd tenses- 63-I-Haber +Past-P		no almorcéis
		no almuercen

82-M-Avergonzar
Note: present. preterite. present subjunctive. imperative.

Verb infinitive	Participles	Imprfect-sub've 1
Avergonzar, to embarrass to shame	avergonzado: avergonzando	yo avergonzara
		tú avergonzaras
Present	**Future**	él avergonzara
yo avergüenzo	yo avergonzaré	n'os avergonzáramos
tú avergüenzas	tú avergonzarás	vos'os avergonzarais
él avergüenza	él avergonzará	ellos avergonzaran
nos'os avergonzamos	n'os avergonzaremos	
vos'os avergonzáis	v'os avergonzaréis	**Imp'fect-sub've 2**
ellos avergüenzan	ellos avergonzarán	yo avergonzase
		tú avergonzases
Imperfect	**Conditional**	él avergonzase
yo avergonzaba	yo avergonzaría	nos'os avergonzásemos
tú avergonzabas	tú avergonzarías	vos'os avergonzaseis
él avergonzaba	él avergonzaría	ellos avergonzasen
nos'os avergonzábamos	nos'os avergonzaríamos	
vos'os avergonzabais	v'os avergonzaríais	**Imperative-Do**
ellos avergonzaban	ellos avergonzarían	(tú) avergüenza
		(él) avergüence
Preterite	**Present subj've**	(nos'os) avergoncemos
yo avergoncé	yo avergüence	(vos'os) avergonzad
tú avergonzaste	tú avergüences	(ellos) avergüencen
él avergonzó	él avergüence	
nos'os avergonzamos	nos'os avergoncemos	**Imperative-Don't**
vos'os avergonzasteis	vos'os avergoncéis	no avergüences
ellos avergonzaron	ellos avergüencen	no avergüence
		no avergoncemos
Comp'nd tenses- 63-I-Haber +Past-P		no avergoncéis
		no avergüencen

83-M-Ceñir

Note: participles. present. preterite. present subjunctive. imperfect-subjunctive. imperative.

Also see/compare verb types: **31-S-Servir-Competir** and **5-O-Bruñir-Tañer**

Verb infinitive	Participles	Imperfect-subjunctive 1
Ceñir, to encircle, to surround, to fit tightly	ceñido: ciñendo	yo ciñera
		tú ciñeras
Present	**Future**	él ciñera
yo ciño	yo ceñiré	nos'os ciñéramos
tú ciñes	tú ceñirás	vos'os ciñerais
él ciñe	él ceñirá	ellos ciñeran
nos'os ceñimos	nos'os ceñiremos	
vos'os ceñís	vos'os ceñiréis	**Imp'fect-sub've 2**
ellos ciñen	ellos ceñirán	yo ciñese
		tú ciñeses
Imperfect	**Conditional**	él ciñese
yo ceñía	yo ceñiría	nos'os ciñésemos
tú ceñías	tú ceñirías	vos'os ciñeseis
él ceñía	él ceñiría	ellos ciñesen
nos'os ceñíamos	nos'os ceñiríamos	
vos'os ceñíais	vos'os ceñiríais	**Imperative-Do**
ellos ceñían	ellos ceñirían	(tú) ciñe
		(él) ciña
Preterite	**Present subj've**	(nos'os) ciñamos
yo ceñí	yo ciña	(vos'os) ceñid
tú ceñiste	tú ciñas	(ellos) ciñan
él ciñó	él ciña	
nos'os ceñimos	nos'os ciñamos	**Imperative-Don't**
vos'os ceñisteis	vos'os ciñáis	no ciñas
ellos ciñeron	ellos ciñan	no ciña
		no ciñamos
Comp'nd tenses- 63-I-Haber +Past-P		no ciñáis
		no ciñan

106

84-M-Colgar

Note: present. preterite. present subjunctive. imperative.
Also see/compare verb types **27-S-Morder-Remover** and **10-O-Pagar**

Verb infinitive	Participles	Imperfect-subjunctive 1
Colgar, to hang	colgado: colgando	yo colgara
		tú colgaras
Present	**Future**	él colgara
yo cuelgo	yo colgaré	nos'os colgáramos
tú cuelgas	tú colgarás	vos'os colgarais
él cuelga	él colgará	ellos colgaran
nos'os colgamos	nos'os colgaremos	
vos'os colgáis	vos'os colgaréis	**Imp'fect-sub've 2**
ellos cuelgan	ellos colgarán	yo colgase
		tú colgases
Imperfect	**Conditional**	él colgase
yo colgaba	yo colgaría	nos'os colgásemos
tú colgabas	tú colgarías	vos'os colgaseis
él colgaba	él colgaría	ellos colgasen
nos'os colgábamos	nos'os colgaríamos	
vos'os colgabais	vos'os colgaríais	**Imperative-Do**
ellos colgaban	ellos colgarían	(tú) cuelga
		(él) cuelgue
Preterite	**Present subj've**	(nos'os) colguemos
yo colgué	yo cuelgue	(vos'os) colgad
tú colgaste	tú cuelgues	(ellos) cuelguen
él colgó	él cuelgue	
nos'os colgamos	nos'os colguemos	**Imperative-Don't**
vos'os colgasteis	vos'os colguéis	no cuelgues
ellos colgaron	ellos cuelguen	no cuelgue
		no colguemos
Comp'nd tenses- 63-I-Haber +Past-P		no colguéis
		no cuelguen

107

85-M-Comenzar

Note: present. present subjunctive. imperative.

Verb infinitive	Participles	Imperfect-subjunctive 1
Colgar, to hang	Comenzado: comenzando	yo comenzara
		tú comenzaras
Present	**Future**	él comenzara
yo comienzo	yo comenzaré	nos'os comenzáramos
tú comienzas	tú comenzarás	vos'os comenzarais
él comienza	él comenzará	ellos comenzaran
nos'os comenzamos	nos'os comenzaremos	
vos'os comenzáis	vos'os comenzaréis	**Imp'fect-sub've 2**
ellos comenzan	ellos comenzarán	yo comenzase
		tú comenzases
Imperfect	**Conditional**	él comenzase
yo comenzaba	yo comenzaría	nos'os comenzásemos
tú comenzabas	tú comenzarías	vos'os comenzaseis
él comenzaba	él comenzaría	ellos comenzasen
nos'os comenzábamos	nos'os comenzaríamos	
vos'os comenzabais	vos'os comenzaríais	**Imperative-Do**
ellos comenzaban	ellos comenzarían	(tú) comienza
		(él) comience
Preterite	**Present subj've**	(nos'os) comencemos
yo comencé	yo comience	(vos'os) comenzad
tú comenzaste	tú comiences	(ellos) comiencen
él comenzó	él comience	
nos'os comenzamos	nos'os comencemos	**Imperative-Don't**
vos'os comenzasteis	vos'os comencéis	no comiences
ellos comenzaron	ellos comiencen	no comience
		no comencemos
Comp'nd tenses- 63-I-Haber +Past-P		no comencéis
		no comiencen

86-M-Empezar

Note: present. preterite. present subjunctive. imperative.
Also see/compare verb types **7-O-Rezar** and **24-S-Alentar-Acertar**

Verb infinitive	Participles	Imperfect-subjunctive 1
Empezar, to begin	empezado: empezando	yo empezara
		tú empezaras
Present	**Future**	él empezara
yo empiezo	yo empezaré	nos'os empezáramos
tú empiezas	tú empezarás	vos'os empezarais
él empieza	él empezará	ellos empezaran
nos'os empezamos	nos'os empezaremos	
vos'os empezáis	vos'os empezaréis	**Imp'fect-sub've 2**
ellos empiezan	ellos empezarán	yo empezase
		tú empezases
Imperfect	**Conditional**	él empezase
yo empezaba	yo empezaría	nos'os empezásemos
tú empezabas	tú empezarías	vos'os empezaseis
él empezaba	él empezaría	ellos empezasen
nos'os empezábamos	nos'os empezaríamos	
vos'os empezabais	vos'os empezaríais	**Imperative-Do**
ellos empezaban	ellos empezarían	(tú) empieza
		(él) empiece
Preterite	**Present subj've**	(nos'os) empecemos
yo empecé	yo empiece	(vos'os) empezad
tú empezaste	tú empieces	(ellos) empiecen
él empezó	él empiece	
nos'os empezamos	nos'os empecemos	**Imperative-Don't**
vos'os empezasteis	vos'os empecéis	no empieces
ellos empezaron	ellos empiecen	no empiece
		no empecemos
Comp'nd tenses- 63-I-Haber +Past-P		no empecéis
		no empiecen

87-M-Forzar
Note: present. preterite. present subjunctive. imperative.
Also see/compare verb types **7-O-Rezar** and **26-S-Aprobar-Acortar**

Verb infinitive	Participles	Imperfect-subjunctive 1
Forzar, to force, to compel	forzado: forzando	yo forzara
		tú forzaras
Present	**Future**	él forzara
yo fuerzo	yo forzaré	nos'os forzáramos
tú fuerzas	tú forzarás	vos'os forzarais
él fuerza	él forzará	ellos forzaran
nos'os forzamos	nos'os forzaremos	
vos'os forzáis	vos'os forzaréis	**Imp'fect-sub've 2**
ellos fuerzan	ellos forzarán	yo forzase
		tú forzases
Imperfect	**Conditional**	él forzase
yo forzaba	yo forzaría	nos'os forzásemos
tú forzabas	tú forzarías	vos'os forzaseis
él forzaba	él forzaría	ellos forzasen
nos'os forzábamos	nos'os forzaríamos	
vos'os forzabais	vos'os forzaríais	**Imperative-Do**
ellos forzaban	ellos forzarían	(tú) fuerza
		(él) fuerce
Preterite	**Present subj've**	(nos'os) forcemos
yo forcé	yo fuerce	(vos'os) forzad
tú forzaste	tú fuerces	(ellos) fuercen
él forzó	él fuerce	
nos'os forzamos	nos'os forcemos	**Imperative-Don't**
vos'os forzasteis	vos'os forcéis	no fuerces
ellos forzaron	ellos fuercen	no fuerce
		no forcemos
Comp'nd tenses- 63-I-Haber +Past-P		no forcéis
		no fuercen

110

88-M-Regar
Note: present. preterite. present subjunctive. imperative.
Also see/compare verb types **10-O-Pagar** and **24-S-Alentar-Acertar**

Verb infinitive	Participles	Imperfect-subjunctive 1
Regar, to water, to irrigate	regado: regando	yo regara
		tú regaras
Present	**Future**	él regara
yo riego	yo regaré	nos'os regáramos
tú riegas	tú regarás	vos'os regarais
él riega	él regará	ellos regaran
nos'os regamos	nos'os regaremos	
vos'os regáis	vos'os regaréis	**Imp'fect-sub've 2**
ellos riegan	ellos regarán	yo regase
		tú regases
Imperfect	**Conditional**	él regase
yo regaba	yo regaría	nos'os regásemos
tú regabas	tú regarías	vos'os regaseis
él regaba	él regaría	ellos regasen
nos'os regábamos	nos'os regaríamos	
vos'os regabais	vos'os regaríais	**Imperative-Do**
ellos regaban	ellos regarían	(tú) riega
		(él) riegue
Preterite	**Present subj've**	(nos'os) reguemos
yo regué	yo riegue	(vos'os) regad
tú regaste	tú riegues	(ellos) rieguen
él regó	él riegue	
nos'os regamos	nos'os reguemos	**Imperative-Don't**
vos'os regasteis	vos'os reguéis	no riegues
ellos regaron	ellos rieguen	no riegue
		no reguemos
Comp'nd tenses-63-I-Haber +Past-P		no reguéis
		no rieguen

111

89-M-Seguir

Note: participles. present. preterite. present subjunctive. imperfect-subjunctive. imperative.

Also see/compare verb types **31-S-Servir-Competir** and **14-O-Distinguir**

Verb infinitive	Participles	Imperfect-subjunctive 1
Seguir, to follow	seguido: siguiendo	yo siguiera
		tú siguieras
Present	**Future**	él siguiera
yo sigo	yo seguiré	nos'os siguiéramos
tú sigues	tú seguirás	vos'os siguierais
él sigue	él seguirá	ellos siguieran
nos'os seguimos	nos'os seguiremos	
vos'os seguís	vos'os seguiréis	**Imp'fect-sub've 2**
ellos siguen	ellos seguirán	yo siguiese
		tú siguieses
Imperfect	**Conditional**	él siguiese
yo seguía	yo seguiría	nos'os siguiésemos
tú seguías	tú seguirías	vos'os siguieseis
él seguía	él seguiría	ellos siguiesen
nos'os seguíamos	nos'os seguiríamos	
vos'os seguíais	vos'os seguiríais	**Imperative-Do**
ellos seguían	ellos seguirían	(tú) sigue
		(él) siga
Preterite	**Present subj've**	(nos'os) sigamos
yo seguí	yo siga	(vos'os) seguid
tú seguiste	tú sigas	(ellos) sigan
él siguió	él siga	
nos'os seguimos	nos'os sigamos	**Imperative-Don't**
vos'os seguisteis	vos'os sigáis	no sigas
ellos siguieron	ellos sigan	no siga
		no sigamos
Comp'nd tenses- 63-I-Haber +Past-P		no sigáis
		no sigan

90-M-Trocar
Note: present. preterite. present subjunctive. imperative.
Also see/compare verb types **9-O-Tocar** and **26-S-Aprobar-Acortar**

Verb infinitive	Participles	Imperfect-subjunctive 1
Trocar, to exchange, to barter	trocado: trocando	yo trocara
		tú trocaras
Present	**Future**	él trocara
yo trueco	yo trocaré	nos'os trocáramos
tú truecas	tú trocarás	vos'os trocarais
él trueca	él trocará	ellos trocaran
nos'os trocamos	nos'os trocaremos	
vos'os trocáis	vos'os trocaréis	**Imp'fect-sub've 2**
ellos truecan	ellos trocarán	yo trocase
		tú trocases
Imperfect	**Conditional**	él trocase
yo trocaba	yo trocaría	nos'os trocásemos
tú trocabas	tú trocarías	vos'os trocaseis
él trocaba	él trocaría	ellos trocasen
nos'os trocábamos	nos'os trocaríamos	
vos'os trocabais	vos'os trocaríais	**Imperative-Do**
ellos trocaban	ellos trocarían	(tú) trueca
		(él) trueque
Preterite	**Present subj've**	(nos'os) troquemos
yo troqué	yo trueque	(vos'os) trocad
tú trocaste	tú trueques	(ellos) truequen
él trocó	él trueque	
nos'os trocamos	nos'os troquemos	**Imperative-Don't**
vos'os trocasteis	vos'os troquéis	no trueques
ellos trocaron	ellos truequen	no trueque
		no troquemos
Comp'nd tenses- 63-I-Haber +Past-P		no troquéis
		no truequen

91- Ú/Í -Evaluar

Note: present. present subjunctive. imperative.

Verb infinitive	Participles	Imperfect-subjunctive 1
Evaluar, to evaluate.	evaluado: evaluando	yo evaluara
		tú evaluaras
Present	**Future**	él evaluara
yo evalúo	yo evaluaré	nos'os evaluáramos
tú evalúas	tú evaluarás	vos'os evaluarais
él evalúa	él evaluará	ellos evaluaran
nos'os evaluamos	nos'os evaluaremos	
vos'os evaluáis	vos'os evaluaréis	**Imp'fect-sub've 2**
ellos evalúan	ellos evaluarán	yo evaluase
		tú evaluases
Imperfect	**Conditional**	él evaluase
yo evaluaba	yo evaluaría	nos'os evaluásemos
tú evaluabas	tú evaluarías	vos'os evaluaseis
él evaluaba	él evaluaría	ellos evaluasen
nos'os evaluábamos	nos'os evaluaríamos	
vos'os evaluabais	vos'os evaluaríais	**Imperative-Do**
ellos evaluaban	ellos evaluarían	(tú) evalúa
		(él) evalúe
Preterite	**Present subj've**	(nos'os) evaluemos
yo evalué	yo evalúe	(vos'os) evaluad
tú evaluaste	tú evalúes	(ellos) evalúen
él evaluó	él evalúe	
nos'os evaluamos	nos'os evaluemos	**Imperative-Don't**
vos'os evaluasteis	vos'os evaluéis	no evalúes
ellos evaluaron	ellos evalúen	no evalúe
		no evaluemos
Comp'nd tenses-63-I-Haber +Past-P		no evaluéis
		no evalúen

114

92-Ú/Í-Ampliar

Note. present. present subjunctive. imperative.

Verb infinitive	Participles	Imperfect-subjunctive 1
Ampliar, to extend, to amplify	ampliado: ampliando	yo ampliara
		tú ampliaras
Present	**Future**	él ampliara
yo amplío	yo ampliaré	nos'os ampliáramos
tú amplías	tú ampliarás	vos'os ampliarais
él amplía	él ampliará	ellos ampliaran
nos'os ampliamos	nos'os ampliaremos	
vos'os ampliáis	vos'os ampliaréis	**Imp'fect-sub've 2**
ellos amplían	ellos ampliarán	yo ampliase
		tú ampliases
Imperfect	**Conditional**	él ampliase
yo ampliaba	yo ampliaría	nos'os ampliásemos
tú ampliabas	tú ampliarías	vos'os ampliaseis
él ampliaba	él ampliaría	ellos ampliasen
nos'os ampliábamos	nos'os ampliaríamos	
vos'os ampliabais	vos'os ampliaríais	**Imperative-Do**
ellos ampliaban	ellos ampliarían	(tú) amplía
		(él) amplíe
Preterite	**Present subj've**	(nos'os) ampliemos
yo amplié	yo amplíe	(vos'os) ampliad
tú ampliaste	tú amplíes	(ellos) amplíen
él amplió	él amplíe	
nos'os ampliamos	nos'os ampliemos	**Imperative-Don't**
vos'os ampliasteis	vos'os ampliéis	no amplíes
ellos ampliaron	ellos amplíen	no amplíe
		no ampliemos
Comp'nd tenses- 63-I-Haber +Past-P		no ampliéis
		no amplíen

93-Ú/Í-Aullar

Note: present. present subjunctive.. imperative.

Verb infinitive	Participles	Imperfect-subjunctive 1
Aullar, to howl, to yell	aullado: aullando	yo aullara
		tú aullaras
Present	**Future**	él aullara
yo aúllo	yo aullaré	nos'os aulláramos
tú aúllas	tú aullarás	vos'os aullarais
él aúlla	él aullará	ellos aullaran
nos'os aullamos	nos'os aullaremos	
vos'os aulláis	vos'os aullaréis	**Imp'fect-sub've 2**
ellos aúllan	ellos aullarán	yo aullase
		tú aullases
Imperfect	**Conditional**	él aullase
yo aullaba	yo aullaría	nos'os aullásemos
tú aullabas	tú aullarías	vos'os aullaseis
él aullaba	él aullaría	
nos'os aullábamos	nos'os aullaríamos	
vos'os aullabais	vos'os aullaríais	**Imperative-Do**
ellos aullaban	ellos aullarían	(tú) aúlla
		(él) aúlle
Preterite	**Present subj've**	(nos'os) aullemos
yo aullé	yo aúlle	(vos'os) aullad
tú aullaste	tú aúlles	(ellos) aúllen
él aulló	él aúlle	
nos'os aullamos	nos'os aullemos	**Imperative-Don't**
vos'os aullasteis	vos'os aulléis	no aúlles
ellos aullaron	ellos aúllen	no aúlle
		no aullemos
Comp'nd tenses-63-I-Haber +Past-P		no aulléis
		no aúllen

94-Ú/Í-Airar

Note: present. present subjunctive. imperative

Verb infinitive	Participles	Imperfect-subjunctive 1
Airar, to annoy, to irritate	airado: airando	yo airara
		tú airaras
Present	**Future**	él airara
yo aíro	yo airaré	nos'os airáramos
tú aíras	tú airarás	vos'os airarais
él aíra	él airará	ellos airaran
nos'os airamos	nos'os airaremos	
vos'os airáis	vos'os airaréis	**Imp'fect-sub've 2**
ellos aíran	ellos airarán	yo airase
		tú airases
Imperfect	**Conditional**	él airase
yo airaba	yo airaría	nos'os airásemos
tú airabas	tú airarías	vos'os airaseis
él airaba	él airaría	ellos airasen
nos'os airábamos	nos'os airaríamos	
vos'os airabais	vos'os airaríais	**Imperative-Do**
ellos airaban	ellos airarían	(tú) aíra
		(él) aíre
Preterite	**Present subj've**	(nos'os) airemos
yo airé	yo aíre	(vos'os) airad
tú airaste	tú aíres	(ellos) aíren
él airó	él aíre	
nos'os airamos	nos'os airemos	**Imperative-Don't**
vos'os airasteis	vos'os airéis	no aíres
ellos airaron	ellos aíren	no aíre
		no airemos
Comp'nd tenses- 63-I-Haber +Past-P		no airéis
		no aíren

117

95-Ú/Í-Rehusar

Note: present. present subjunctive. imperative.

Verb infinitive	Participles	Imperfect-subjunctive 1
Rehusar, to decline, to refuse.	rehusado: rehusando	yo rehusara
		tú rehusaras
Present	**Future**	él rehusara
yo rehúso	yo rehusaré	nos'os rehusáramos
tú rehúsas	tú rehusarás	vos'os rehusarais
él rehúsa	él rehusará	ellos rehusaran
nos'os rehusamos	nos'os rehusaremos	
vos'os rehusáis	vos'os rehusaréis	**Imp'fect-sub've 2**
ellos rehúsan	ellos rehusarán	yo rehusase
		tú rehusases
Imperfect	**Conditional**	él rehusase
yo rehusaba	yo rehusaría	nos'os rehusásemos
tú rehusabas	tú rehusarías	vos'os rehusaseis
él rehusaba	él rehusaría	ellos rehusasen
nos'os rehusábamos	nos'os rehusaríamos	
vos'os rehusabais	vos'os rehusaríais	**Imperative-Do**
ellos rehusaban	ellos rehusarían	(tú) rehúsa
		(él) rehúse
Preterite	**Present subj've**	(nos'os) rehusemos
yo rehusé	yo rehúse	(vos'os) rehusad
tú rehusaste	tú rehúses	(ellos) rehúsen
él rehusó	él rehúse	
nos'os rehusamos	nos'os rehusemos	**Imperative-Don't**
vos'os rehusasteis	vos'os rehuséis	no rehúses
ellos rehusaron	ellos rehúsen	no rehúse
		no rehusemos
Comp'nd tenses-63-I-Haber +Past-P		no rehuséis
		no rehúsen

118

96-Ú/Í-Prohibir

Note: present. present subjunctive. imperative

Verb infinitive	Participles	Imperfect-subjunctive 1
prohibir, to forbid, to prohibit	prohibido: prohibiendo	yo prohibiera
		tú prohibieras
Present	**Future**	él prohibiera
yo prohíbo	yo prohibiré	nos'os prohibiéramos
tú prohíbes	tú prohibirás	vos'os prohibierais
él prohíbe	él prohibirá	ellos prohibieran
nos'os prohibimos	nos'os prohibiremos	
vos'os prohibís	vos'os prohibiréis	**Imp'fect-sub've 2**
ellos prohíben	ellos prohibirán	yo prohibiese
		tú prohibieses
Imperfect	**Conditional**	él prohibiese
yo prohibía	yo prohibiría	nos'os prohibiésemos
tú prohibías	tú prohibirías	vos'os prohibieseis
él prohibía	él prohibiría	ellos prohibiesen
nos'os prohibíamos	nos'os prohibiríamos	
vos'os prohibíais	vos'os prohibiríais	**Imperative-Do**
ellos prohibían	ellos prohibirían	(tú) prohíbe
		(él) prohíba
Preterite	**Present subj've**	(nos'os) prohibamos
yo prohibí	yo prohíba	(vos'os) prohibid
tú prohibiste	tú prohíbas	(ellos) prohíban
él prohibió	él prohíba	
nos'os prohibimos	nos'os prohibamos	**Imperative-Don't**
vos'os prohibisteis	vos'os prohibáis	no prohíbas
ellos prohibieron	ellos prohíban	no prohíba
		no prohibamos
Comp'nd tenses-63-I-Haber +Past-P		no prohibáis
		no prohíban

119

97-Ú/Í-Reunir

Note: present. present subjunctive. imperative

Verb infinitive	Participles	Imperfect-subjunctive 1
Reunir, to assemble, to gather	reunido reuniendo	yo reuniera
		tú reunieras
Present	**Future**	él reuniera
yo reúno	yo reuniré	nos'os reuniéramos
tú reúnes	tú reunirás	vos'os reunierais
él reúne	él reunirá	ellos reunieran
nos'os reunimos	nos'os reuniremos	
vos'os reunís	vos'os reuniréis	**Imp'fect-sub've 2**
ellos reúnen	ellos reunirán	yo reuniese
		tú reunieses
Imperfect	**Conditional**	él reuniese
yo reunía	yo reuniría	nos'os reuniésemos
tú reunías	tú reunirías	vos'os reunieseis
él reunía	él reuniría	ellos reuniesen
nos'os reuníamos	nos'os reuniríamos	
vos'os reuníais	vos'os reuniríais	**Imperative-Do**
ellos reunían	ellos reunirían	(tú) reúne
		(él) reúna
Preterite	**Present subj've**	(nos'os) reunamos
yo reuní	yo reúna	(vos'os) reunid
tú reuniste	tú reúnas	(ellos) reúnan
él reunió	él reúna	
nos'os reunimos	nos'os reunamos	**Imperative-Don't**
vos'os reunisteis	vos'os reunáis	no reúnas
ellos reunieron	ellos reúnan	no reúna
		no reunamos
Comp'nd tenses- 63-I-Haber +Past-P		no reunáis
		no reúnan

98-Ú/Í-Atraillar

Note: present. present subjunctive. imperative

Verb infinitive	Participles	Imperfect-subjunctive 1
atraillar, to put on a leash	atraillado atraillando	yo atraillara
		tú atraillaras
Present	**Future**	él atraillara
yo atraíllo	yo atraillaré	nos'os atrailláramos
tú atraíllas	tú atraillarás	vos'os atraillarais
él atraílla	él atraillará	ellos atraillaran
nos'os atraillamos	nos'os atraillaremos	
vos'os atrailláis	vos'os atraillaréis	**Imp'fect-sub've 2**
ellos atraíllan	ellos atraillarán	yo atraillase
		tú atraillases
Imperfect	**Conditional**	él atraillase
yo atraillaba	yo atraillaría	nos'os atraillásemos
tú atraillabas	tú atraillarías	vos'os atraillaseis
é atraillaba	é atraillaría	ellos atraillasen
nos'os atraillábamos	nos'os atraillaríamos	
vos'os atraillabais	vos'os atraillaríais	**Imperative-Do**
ellos atraillaban	ellos atraillarían	(tú) atraílla
		(él) atraílle
Preterite	**Present subj've**	(nos'os) atraillemos
yo atraillé	yo atraílle	(vos'os) atraillad
tú atraillaste	tú atraílles	(ellos) atraíllen
él atrailló	él atraílle	
nos'os atraillamos	nos'os atraillemos	**Imperative-Don't**
vos'os atraillasteis	vos'os atrailléis	no atraílles
ellos atraillaron	ellos atraíllen	no atraílle
		no atraillemos
Comp'nd tenses- 63-I-Haber +Past-P		no atrailléis
		no atraíllen

99-DC-Deshacer

Verb infinitive	Participles	Imperfect-subjunctive 1
deshacer, to undo	deshecho: deshaciendo	yo deshiciera
		tú deshicieras
Present	**Future**	él deshiciera
yo deshago	yo desharé	nos'os deshiciéramos
tú deshaces	tú desharás	vos'os deshicierais
él deshace	é deshará	ellos deshicieran
nos'os deshacemos	nos'os desharemos	
vos'os deshacéis	vos'os desharéis	**Imp'fect-sub've 2**
ellos deshacen	ellos desharán	yo deshiciese
		tú deshicieses
Imperfect	**Conditional**	él deshiciese
yo deshacía	yo desharía	nos'os deshiciésemos
tú deshacías	tú desharías	vos'os deshicieseis
él deshacía	él desharía	ellos deshiciesen
nos'os deshacíamos	nos'os desharíamos	
vos'os deshacíais	vos'os desharíais	**Imperative-Do**
ellos deshacían	ellos desharían	(tú) deshaz
		(él) deshaga
Preterite	**Present subj've**	(nos'os) deshagamos
yo deshice	yo deshaga	(vos'os) deshaced
tú deshiciste	tú deshagas	(ellos) deshagan
él deshizo	él deshaga	
nos'os deshicimos	nos'os deshagamos	**Imperative-Don't**
vos'os deshicisteis	vos'os deshagáis	no deshagas
ellos deshicieron	ellos deshagan	no deshaga
		no deshagamos
Comp'nd tenses-63-I-Haber +Past-P		no deshagáis
		no deshagan

100-DC-Componer

Verb infinitive	Participles	Imperfect-subjunctive 1
componer to put together	compuesto: componiendo	yo compusiera
		tú compusieras
Present	**Future**	él compusiera
yo compongo	yo compondré	nos'os compusiéramos
tú compones	tú compondrás	vos'os compusierais
él compone	él compondrá	ellos compusieran
nos'os componemos	nos'os compondremos	
vos'os componéis	vos'os compondréis	**Imp'fect-sub've 2**
ellos componen	ellos compondrán	yo compusiese
		tú compusieses
Imperfect	**Conditional**	él compusiese
yo componía	yo compondría	nos'os compusiésemos
tú componías	tú compondrías	vos'os compusieseis
él componía	él compondría	ellos compusiesen
nos'os componíamos	nos'os compondríamos	
vos'os componíais	vos'os compondríais	**Imperative-Do**
ellos componían	ellos compondrían	(tú) compón
		(él) componga
Preterite	**Present subj've**	(nos'os) compongamos
yo compuse	yo componga	(vos'os) componed
tú compusiste	tú compongas	(ellos) compongan
él compuso	él componga	
nos'os compusimos	nos'os compongamos	**Imperative-Don't**
vos'os compusisteis	vos'os compongáis	no compongas
ellos compusieron	ellos compongan	no componga
		no compongamos
Comp'nd tenses- 63-I-Haber +Past-P		no compongáis
		no compongan

101-DC-Sobresalir

Verb infinitive	Participles	Imperfect-subjunctive 1
sobresalir, to project, to stand out	sobresalido: sobresaliendo	yo sobresaliera
		tú sobresalieras
Present	**Future**	él sobresaliera
yo sobresalgo	yo sobresaldré	nos'os sobresaliéramos
tú sobresales	tú sobresaldrás	vos'os sobresalierais
él sobresale	él sobresaldrá	ellos sobresalieran
nos'os sobresalimos	nos'os sobresaldremos	
vos'os sobresalís	vos'os sobresaldréis	**Imp'fect-sub've 2**
ellos sobresalen	ellos sobresaldrán	yo sobresaliese
		tú sobresalieses
Imperfect	**Conditional**	él sobresaliese
yo sobresalía	yo sobresaldría	nos'os sobresaliésemos
tú sobresalías	tú sobresaldrías	vos'os sobresalieseis
él sobresalía	él sobresaldría	ellos sobresaliesen
nos'os sobresalíamos	nos'os sobresaldríamos	
vos'os sobresalíais	vos'os sobresaldríais	**Imperative-Do**
ellos sobresalían	ellos sobresaldrían	(tú) sobresal
		(él) sobresalga
Preterite	**Present subj've**	(nos'os) sobresalgamos
yo sobresalí	yo sobresalga	(vos'os) sobresalid
tú sobresaliste	tú sobresalgas	(ellos) sobresalgan
él sobresalió	él sobresalga	
nos'os sobresalimos	nos'os sobresalgamos	**Imperative-Don't**
vos'os sobresalisteis	vos'os sobresalgáis	no sobresalgas
ellos sobresalieron	ellos sobresalgan	no sobresalga
		no sobresalgamos
Comp'nd tenses-63-I-Haber +Past-P		no sobresalgáis
		no sobresalgan

102-DC-Equivaler

Verb infinitive	Participles	Imperfect-subjunctive 1
equivaler, to be equal to	equivalido: equivaliendo	yo equivaliera
		tú equivalieras
Present	**Future**	él equivaliera
yo equivalgo	yo equivaldré	nos'os equivaliéramos
tú equivales	tú equivaldrás	vos'os equivalierais
él equivale	él equivaldrá	ellos equivalieran
nos'os equivalemos	nos'os equivaldremos	
vos'os equivaléis	vos'os equivaldréis	**Imp'fect-sub've 2**
ellos equivalen	ellos equivaldrán	yo equivaliese
		tú equivalieses
Imperfect	**Conditional**	él equivaliese
yo equivalía	yo equivaldría	nos'os equivaliésemos
tú equivalías	tú equivaldrías	vos'os equivalieseis
él equivalía	él equivaldría	ellos equivaliesen
nos'os equivalíamos	nos'os equivaldríamos	
vos'os equivalíais	vos'os equivaldríais	**Imperative-Do**
ellos equivalían	ellos equivaldrían	(tú) equivale
		(él) equivalga
Preterite	**Present subj've**	(nos'os) equivalgamos
yo equivalí	yo equivalga	(vos'os) equivaled
tú equivaliste	tú equivalgas	(ellos) equivalgan
él equivalió	él equivalga	
nos'os equivalimos	nos'os equivalgamos	**Imperative-Don't**
vos'os equivalisteis	vos'os equivalgáis	no equivalgas
ellos equivalieron	ellos equivalgan	no equivalga
		no equivalgamos
Comp'nd tenses- 63-I-Haber +Past-P		no equivalgáis
		no equivalgan

103-DC-Retraer

Verb infinitive	Participles	Imperfect-subjunctive 1
retraer, to draw in, to retract	retraído: retrayendo	**yo retrajera**
		tú re**trajeras**
Present	**Future**	él re**trajera**
yo retraigo	yo retraeré	nos'os re**trajéramos**
tú retraes	tú retraerás	vos'os re**trajerais**
él retrae	él retraerá	ellos re**trajeran**
nos'os retraemos	nos'os retraeremos	
vos'os retraéis	vos'os retraeréis	**Imp'fect-sub've 2**
ellos retraen	ellos retraerán	yo retrajese
		tú retrajeses
Imperfect	**Conditional**	él retrajese
yo retraía	yo retraería	nos'os retrajésemos
tú retraías	tú retraerías	vos'os retrajeseis
él retraía	él retraería	ellos retrajesen
nos'os retraíamos	nos'os retraeríamos	
vos'os retraíais	vos'os retraeríais	**Imperative-Do**
ellos retraían	ellos retraerían	(tú) retrae
		(él) retraiga
Preterite	**Present subj've**	(nos'os) retraigamos
yo retraje	yo retraiga	(vos'os) retraed
tú retrajiste	tú retraigas	(ellos) retraigan
él retrajo	él retraiga	
nos'os retrajimos	nos'os retraigamos	**Imperative-Don't**
vos'os retrajisteis	vos'os retraigáis	no retraigas
ellos retrajeron	ellos retraigan	no retraiga
		no retraigamos
Comp'nd tenses-63-I-Haber +Past-P		no retraigáis
		no retraigan

126

104-DC-Convenir

Verb infinitive	Participles	Imperfect-subjunctive 1
convenir, to agree, to suit	convenido: conviniendo	yo conviniera
		tú convinieras
Present	**Future**	él conviniera
yo convengo	yo convendré	nos'os conviniéramos
tú convienes	tú convendrás	vos'os convinierais
él conviene	él convendrá	ellos convinieran
nos'os convenimos	nos'os convendremos	
vos'os convenís	vos'os convendréis	**Imp'fect-sub've 2**
ellos convienen	ellos convendrán	yo conviniese
		tú convinieses
Imperfect	**Conditional**	él conviniese
yo convenía	yo convendría	nos'os conviniésemos
tú convenías	tú convendrías	vos'os convinieseis
él convenía	él convendría	ellos conviniesen
nos'os conveníamos	nos'os convendríamos	
vos'os conveníais	vos'os convendríais	**Imperative-Do**
ellos convenían	ellos convendrían	(tú) convén
		(él) convenga
Preterite	**Present subj've**	(nos'os) convengamos
yo convine	yo convenga	(vos'os) convenid
tú conviniste	tú convengas	(ellos) convengan
él convino	él convenga	
nos'os convinimos	nos'os convengamos	**Imperative-Don't**
vos'os convinisteis	vos'os convengáis	no convengas
ellos convinieron	ellos convengan	no convenga
		no convengamos
Comp'nd tenses- 63-I-Haber +Past-P		no convengáis
		no convengan

127

105-DC-Prever

Verb infinitive	Participles	Imperfect-subjunctive 1
prever, to foresee, to anticipate	previsto: previendo	yo previera
		tú previeras
Present	**Future**	él previera
yo preveo	yo preveré	nos'os previéramos
tú preves	tú preverás	vos'os previerais
él preve	él preverá	ellos previeran
nos'os prevemos	nos'os preveremos	
vos'os preveis	vos'os preveréis	**Imp'fect-sub've 2**
ellos preven	ellos preverán	yo previese
		tú previeses
Imperfect	**Conditional**	él previese
yo preveía	yo prevería	nos'os previésemos
tú preveías	tú preverías	vos'os previeseis
él preveía	él prevería	ellos previesen
nos'os preveíamos	nos'os preveríamos	
vos'os preveíais	vos'os preveríais	**Imperative-Do**
ellos preveían	ellos preverían	(tú) preve
		(él) prevea
Preterite	**Present subj've**	(nos'os) preveamos
yo preví	yo prevea	(vos'os) preved
tú previste	tú preveas	(ellos) prevean
él previó	él prevea	
nos'os previmos	nos'os preveamos	**Imperative-Don't**
vos'os previsteis	vos'os preveáis	no preveas
ellos previeron	ellos prevean	no prevea
		no preveamos
Comp'nd tenses-63-I-Haber +Past-P		no preveáis
		no prevean

128

106-D-R-S- Costar
Verb only exists in third persons singular and plural

Verb infinitive	Participles	Imperfect-subjunctive 1
Costar: to cost	Costado: costando	que costara
		que costaran
Present	**Future**	
cuesta	costará	**Imp'fect-sub've 2**
cuestan	costarán	que costase
		que costasen
Imperfect	**Conditional**	
costaba	costaría	**Imperative**
costaban	costarían	que cueste
		que cuesten
Preterite	**Present subj've**	
costó	que cueste	
costaron	que cuesten	
Comp'nd tenses-	**Single**	**Plural**
Present perfect	ha + Past P	han+ Past P
Pluperfect	había+ Past P	habían+ Past P
Preterite perfect	hubo + Past P	hubieron+ Past P
Future perfect	habrá+ Past P	habrán+ Past P
Conditional perfect	habría+ Past P	habrían+ Past P
Present perfect subjv	haya+ Past P	hayan+ Past P
Pluperfect subjv 1	hubiera + Past P	hubieran+ Past P
Pluperfect subjv 2	hubiese + Past P	hubiesen+ Past P

107-D-R- Encantar
Verb only exists in third persons singular and plural

Verb infinitive	Participles	Imperfect-subjunctive 1
Encantar : to delight	Encantado: Encantando	encantara
		encantaran
Present	**Future**	
encanta	encantará	**Imp'fect-sub've 2**
encantan	encantarán	encantase
		encantasen
Imperfect	**Conditional**	
encantaba	encantaría	**Imperative**
encantaban	encantarían	encante
		encanten
Preterite	**Present subj've**	
encantó	encante	
encantaron	encanten	

Comp'nd tenses-	Single	Plural
Present perfect	ha + Past P	han+ Past P
Pluperfect	había+ Past P	habían+ Past P
Preterite perfect	hubo + Past P	hubieron+ Past P
Future perfect	habrá+ Past P	habrán+ Past P
Conditional perfect	habría+ Past P	habrían+ Past P
Present perfect subjv	haya+ Past P	hayan+ Past P
Pluperfect subjv 1	hubiera + Past P	hubieran+ Past P
Pluperfect subjv 2	hubiese + Past P	hubiesen+ Past P

108-D-R-Gustar
Verb only exists in third persons singular and plural

Verb infinitive	Participles	Imperfect-subjunctive 1
Gustar: to be pleasing to, to like	Gustado: Gustando	gustara
		gustaran
Present	**Future**	
gusta	gustará	**Imp'fect-sub've 2**
gustan	gustaran	gustase
		gustasen
Imperfect	**Conditional**	
gustaba	gustaría	**Imperative**
gustaban	gustarían	guste
		gusten
Preterite	**Present subj've**	
gustó	guste	
gustaron	gusten	
Comp'nd tenses-	**Single**	**Plural**
Present perfect	ha + Past P	han+ Past P
Pluperfect	había+ Past P	habían+ Past P
Preterite perfect	hubo + Past P	hubieron+ Past P
Future perfect	habrá+ Past P	habrán+ Past P
Conditional perfect	habría+ Past P	habrían+ Past P
Present perfect subjv	haya+ Past P	hayan+ Past P
Pluperfect subjv 1	hubiera + Past P	hubieran+ Past P
Pluperfect subjv 2	hubiese + Past P	hubiesen+ Past P

109-D-S – Llover
Verb only exists in third person singular

Verb infinitive	Participles	Imperfect-subjunctive 1
Llover: to rain	Llovido: Lloviendo	lloviera
Present	**Future**	
llueve	lloverá	**Imp'fect-sub've 2**
		lloviese
Imperfect	**Conditional**	
llovía	llovería	**Imperative**
		llueva
Preterite	**Present subj've**	
llovió	llueva	
Comp'nd tenses-	**Single**	
Present perfect	ha + Past P	
Pluperfect	había+ Past P	
Preterite perfect	hubo + Past P	
Future perfect	habrá+ Past P	
Conditional perfect	habría+ Past P	
Present perfect subjv	haya+ Past P	
Pluperfect subjv 1	hubiera + Past P	
Pluperfect subjv 2	hubiese + Past P	

Note: the Future and Conditional Tenses

Verbs which are irregular in the future and conditional tenses

The number of Spanish verbs which are irregular in the future tense is limited to just the twelve below (there are no others) and all are easy to learn. Moreover the irregularity does not relate to the endings for the future tense but to what would otherwise be the infinitive form to which they are attached. As will be seen from the following comprehensive list, the irregularities mostly consist of the dropping of the final vowel for some of the infinitives, or the replacement of the vowel with the letter d, and in only two cases, decir and hacer, does the stem change completely.

Exactly the same changes occur for the conditional tense and so in the following table both the future and the conditional are shown. For each verb just the conjugation for the first person singular (yo) is given. All the other persons have exactly the same variation to the infinitive stem.

Infinitive	Future (yo)	Conditional (yo)
Decir	dir-é	dir-ía
Poner	pondr-é	pondr-ía
Salir	saldr-é	saldr-ía
Valer	valdr-é	valdr-ía
Querer	querr-é	querr-ía
Tener	tendr-é	tendr-ía
Hacer	har-é	har-ía
Haber	habr-é	habr-ía
Poder	podr-é	podr-ía
Saber	sabr-é	sabr-ía
Caber	cabr-é	cabr-ía
Venir	vendr-é	vendr-ía

Note: the Imperfect Tense
The imperfect tense is completely regular for **all** Spanish verbs except for Ir (to go), Ver (to see) and Ser (to be).

The conjugations for these 3 verbs in the imperfect are as follows:-

Imperfect	Ser (to be)	Ver (to see)	Ir (to go)
Yo	era	veía	iba
Tú	eras	veías	ibas
Él/Ella/Ud.	era	veía	iba
Nosotros/as	éramos	veíamos	íbamos
Vosotros/as	erais	veíais	ibais
Ellos/as/Uds.	eran	veían	iban

Conclusion
Good luck with your Spanish studies; and if you have found this book helpful please would you leave a positive review.

These are some of my other books:
How to learn - Spanish - French - German - Arabic - any foreign language successfully.
and
How To Transform Your Memory & Brain Power: Power-Learn, Memorize & Remember Anything.
and
How I Learned To Speak Spanish Fluently In Three Months: Discover How You Can Conquer Spanish Easily The Same Way.
and
Dual Language First Spanish Reader. Spanish-English Short Stories for Beginners
and
Dual Language Spanish Reader. Parallel Spanish-English Short Stories. Level Beginner to Intermediate
and
Spanish Verbs Genius: Everything you need to conquer Spanish verbs and Speak Spanish correctly

.

Printed in Great Britain
by Amazon

37874657R00078